T0153538

RÉN

Published by Welbeck
An imprint of Welbeck Non-Fiction Limited,
part of Welbeck Publishing Group.
20 Mortimer Street,
London W1T 3JW

First published by Welbeck in 2022

A CIP catalogue record for this book is available from
the British Library

ISBN
Hardback – 9781787398221

Typeset by D2P
Printed in China

10 9 8 7 6 5 4 3 2 1

www.welbeckpublishing.com

RÉN

The Ancient
Chinese Art of
Finding Peace
and Fulfilment

Yen Ooi

WELBECK

仁君
艺法

Like all journeys of self-discovery and self-improvement, learning about Rén and practising to become Rén will precipitate highs and lows, emotionally and mentally. This book sets out as a guide to support your self-practice, but do note that it is not a substitute for professional and medical help. Embark on your journey with honesty – listen to your body and mind. Be patient and kind to yourself, and if at any point you feel helpless or you notice you are bringing up a lot of negativity, give yourself permission to seek appropriate professional medical advice. Taking care of ourselves – both physically and mentally – is a part of the journey too.

CONTENTS

10   Introduction

15   Confucius and *The Analects*

19   What is Rén 仁?

PART ONE: Rén and You

37   Taking Care of Ourselves

76   Understanding Being Human

PART TWO: Rén and Family and Friends

115   Understanding Positions and Relationships

131   Rén at Home

142   Rén at Work

157   Rén and Friends

PART THREE: Rén, Society and the Wider World

181   Rén Values

204   On Politics

PART FOUR: Rén Today

223   Rén in the Twenty-first Century

249   Conclusion

253   Acknowledgements

INTRODUCTION

Rén is most beautiful. If we are wise,
when there is a choice, why would we not
choose Rén?

THE ANALECTS 4:1

Growing up in Malaysia, my life began in a multicultural world filled with an array of stories, traditions and philosophies that complemented as well as contradicted one another. Born to parents who are Chinese (my father is first-generation Malaysian), I've now come to realise as an adult that much of my family's own traditions and philosophies are based on cultural practices that were inherited and kept to help us grow and flourish in new environments that may be different from our ancestors' homes. Some would remind us of our ancestors' practices in the past, in a different country, while others would act as a guide for us to follow, to be a better person, as a family member, friend, colleague and member of society. Without being too familiar with local culture and practices, my parents and their parents and siblings had to rely on their upbringing and the inherited knowledge to navigate the world around them and in turn passed this down to me and my sister, Sen.

Even as a child, I had heard of the Chinese philosopher Confucius (c. 551 to c. 479 BCE). Back then, I knew of him as someone important from ancient China (I had no idea then *how* ancient!) who was like a teacher, who said many things that were insightful and that people still respected and followed in our modern day. To my young mind, he was in the same ranks as Shakespeare. As I grew up, I understood a bit more about philosophy, but Confucius jokes in English also became popular and parody proverbs caught on. My favourite one is: *The man who runs in front of car, gets tired. The man who runs behind car, gets exhausted.* They were fun and clearly stayed with me, but they also made it hard for me to consider Confucius's teachings seriously at the time.

In 1997, I moved to the UK for my higher education and it was then that I began to be aware of my own philosophy and ethics. As my parents and grandparents experienced before me, being in a new environment highlighted the differences between my practices and those performed in the world around me. These included how I managed myself under stress, how I reacted to certain socio-political issues, what communities I aligned myself with, how I made career decisions and how I saw myself contributing to the world around me. None of the answers to these questions are fixed. They would change year to-year, or even more frequently, and it is through these changes that my eyes were opened to how we interact with the world around us and how this directly impacts our happiness.

Not long after university, I married and my husband, Kenneth, and we settled down to a new life together in London. Later, we moved to Tokyo for his work assignment, where we lived for three years, which brought on further change. Though I found some similarities with my Chinese and Malaysian cultural heritage, much of it was still completely new and different. The Japanese language was the most distinguishing factor, with concepts of hierarchy that affect word choices and conjugations depending on whom we are speaking to. Though concepts of hierarchy and status in society are similar in Chinese and Malaysian culture, seeing it embedded in the language was something new. We were given cultural lessons in our first weeks there, which really helped with our understanding of the country and opened our eyes to local practices that might have felt odd otherwise. A wonderful example is *tatemae* – a form of 'white lie' used in conversation to be polite and make the other person feel good.

What my three years in Tokyo taught me was to look further into my own practices – which stemmed from my beliefs, philosophy, tradition and culture, and helped me find fulfilment and happiness – to understand how they might be analysed and perhaps even explained to others. It was also in Japan that I changed career paths and became a writer and this provided me with a wonderful canvas to explore cultures, traditions and philosophies in a way that I couldn't before – through storytelling.

On our return to London, I decided to pursue my postgraduate education while developing my writing career, which is what triggered my recent re-encounter with Confucius. Since 2014, I have been studying literature that is culturally recognisable as Chinese and in doing so, I found myself engaging with Confucius's teachings over and over again. This time around, I noticed that in fiction, Chinese cultural values that are presented aren't that different from people's shared cultural practices, like traditions, events, rites and rituals. And where we find similarities in cultural practices or philosophy among East Asian and South East Asian heritage, it can often be traced back to teachings from ancient China that originate in Confucianism, Buddhism and Daoism. This has made me increasingly curious to find out one thing: with the world seeming so different in the twenty-first century, are these teachings still relevant?

Returning to Confucius's teachings anew, I began to see that his philosophy is all-encompassing, a guide to life that helps achieve a sense of happiness, contentment and love. His philosophy is organised into five virtues: Rén 仁 (humanity), Yì 義 (righteousness), Lǐ 禮 (rites), Zhì 智

(wisdom) and Xìn 信 (honesty). The translations I chose here are slightly different from what you might read elsewhere, but I feel that they reflect his core teachings better and are more applicable to our daily lives. The most important one – Rén – sets out to show us how to find fulfilment through our interactions and engagement with the world we live in. Many of the teachings in Rén are familiar to me as they were lessons and practices that I had learnt from my parents and grandparents. Though it was originally through my cultural heritage that my journey with Rén began, I'm glad that I found my way back to Confucius again and that I had the opportunity to study Rén more formally and intimately in recent years. It made me understand the unique value of Confucius's philosophy and helped me uncover the richness of life through the world around me.

This book hopefully captures the essence and philosophy of Rén and its positive message of community and compassion. Organised in four main parts, it begins with Rén and You, then builds outwards to Rén and Family and Friends, then, to Rén, Society and the Wider World and finally, to Rén Today. It contains the lessons, ideas and practices of Rén, all of which helped me navigate the complexities of our modern world and find a new sense of achievement and happiness in life. I hope it will do the same for you too.

YEN OOI
LONDON

CONFUCIUS AND
THE ANALECTS

When walking in company of others, we are
bound to learn something from them.

THE ANALECTS 7:22

Confucius (Kǒng Qiū 孔丘) was a philosopher and teacher
from ancient China. Born c. 551 BCE, his teachings have
been with us for over 2,000 years and in that time, they have
been assimilated into parts of East Asian and South East
Asian culture. In ancient China, the three philosophies and
religions – Confucianism, Daoism and Buddhism – began
their history of mutual influence. Through their shared
history, Confucius's teachings together with Daoism and
Buddhism have lasted in many East and South East Asian
households, where the lessons have been passed down from
generation to generation, often without reference or credit

to Confucius anymore. He has become an integral part of life and culture.

The Analects is a collection of Confucius's teachings and wisdom that he passed on to his students. It was believed to have been compiled by his immediate disciples soon after his death and the disciples helped spread the word over time. The Chinese title, *Lúnyǔ* 論語, means 'a collection of conversations', which explains the dialogue-like quality of the writings. The original books were made of strips of bamboo strung together into accordion-fold collections. The texts were recorded in brush and ink; each strip of bamboo allowed for about two dozen Chinese characters. The full collection is composed of about 500 independent passages divided into 20 such books. Though the texts have been continuously scrutinised by academics and researchers since their publication in ancient China, due to the age of the document there are understandably variances in interpretations and translations, often in an attempt to interpret the texts against modern or current thinking.

In this book, I will be using references from *The Analects* to ground key teachings and I will be doing so with quotations that are adapted for a modernised interpretation that maintains the foundation of the teaching, while allowing its application to be appropriate for engagement today.

Through Rén, Confucius believed in morality, social function, justice, kindness and compassion. Because he understood that our individual identities are actually derived from our interactions within our communities, Confucius saw that the exemplar of humanity would be someone who embraced and practiced these core characteristics – someone who aspires to become Rén. It is here that we can start our journey into understanding our purpose and finding fulfilment through the world around us.

WHAT IS
RÉN 仁?

The wise are not confused, the Rén are
not anxious, the courageous are not afraid.

THE ANALECTS 9:29

RÉN 仁 IS KNOWN in English in many forms. It is
commonly translated as benevolent or humane, kind
or virtuous, but the Chinese character 仁 carries a
lot more meaning than that. To begin to understand Rén
仁, we should look at one of the simplest words in Chinese,
rén 人, which means person. It is written in two strokes and
it depicts a person walking.

Rén 仁 has roots in the word for person, rén 人,
but it also builds upon it. Though they are homophones
(pronounced identically), they are written differently and
carry different meanings.

The Chinese character Rén 仁 is made up of two parts. On the left is the radical rén 亻, which is a simplified version of the character for person rén 人. A radical is used in combination with other characters to form more complex words and the radical would hint to the reader as to the purpose of the word. In this case, a complex word with the radical rén 亻would imply that it has to do with people. To the right of the character Rén 仁 is the character èr 二 for the number two. So essentially the character for Rén is a combination of the characters for person and the number two, thus literally translated as meaning two people and the connection or relationship between two people.

The character èr 二 can also be interpreted visually as a reference to heaven (the top line) and earth (bottom line), which is seen as being a reference to the world. And in this case, the combination of the characters for person and the world could extend to be about our relationship with nature. Taking in both interpretations, Rén 仁 represents the coexistence of people with each other and with the world.

RÉN IS LOVE

When teaching the principles of Rén, Confucius understood that our lives are intricately connected to, and that we coexist with, the world around us. His teachings focus on the action of the individual, but emphasise its impact on

society and nature. He knew that in order for us to thrive as individuals, we need our environment – society and nature – to thrive too. This creates three layers of experience for achieving a positive co-existence:

○ In the first layer, we do something good directly for our own gain. This gives us a sense of accomplishment.

○ In the second layer, we do something good directly for someone else's gain. This gives us a sense of accomplishment and through empathy, we share the other person's happiness.

○ In the third layer, we do something good to improve our environment (from local to international communities and nature). An improved environment allows us to thrive as individuals, which benefits ourselves and others in the affected community.

Knowing that we directly affected a positive change also gives us a sense of accomplishment, which shows how interlinked these three layers are.

The connectedness of experiences we have highlights another translation of Rén 仁, which is 'love' or 'universal love'. Here, 'love' is not a romantic feeling but a need to be kind – to treat everyone and the world around us with basic compassion and care. Because our individual feeling of fulfilment is directly affected by our world, the love of Rén 仁 is both 'human kind' as well as of 'humankind'. Confucius saw love as a fundamental value and reminded us in his teachings that doing good is what we are built for.

WHY DO WE NEED RÉN NOW?

> One who is not Rén can neither be content in poverty nor be happy for long in wealth. The learned are attracted to Rén because they feel at home in it. The wise are attracted to Rén because they find it to their advantage.
>
> THE ANALECTS 4:2

There is no doubt that our lives now in the twenty-first century are a very different experience to those in the fifth century BCE when Confucius was alive. While there has been much development over the 2,000 years in many aspects of the world around us, our fundamental needs and what gives us fulfilment haven't really changed. Learning about the philosophy behind Rén and being guided by Confucius will ground us and give us space to engage with society and nature – and, ultimately, help us to become happier people.

In our fast-paced, technology-laden lives, we are constantly distracted by the day-to-day rhythms of work and social events, often without pause. As a society, we are only now starting to practise more self-care and learning to protect our mental health, but these rituals are often scheduled into our day, like classes or workouts. Much like life itself, Rén requires a lifelong commitment to experience its rewards. Unlike specific mindfulness techniques or self-development courses (which are wonderful and can be undertaken while studying Rén), Rén isn't prescribed through daily routines or progressive exercises. As a philosophy, Rén requires a focus and understanding which through time, engagement and application will grow and strengthen in you.

Having firm and clear ethics drawn from Confucius's teachings of Rén will also alleviate the anxieties of modern social expectations that demand our energy now more than ever before. When engaging with online media and news, we are expected to make regular moral judgements, often without the time or resources to clearly research and understand the issues at stake. Being able to understand how our actions affect ourselves and the world around us through Rén brings reassurance and allows us to contain any doubts and anxieties we might have – a lesson anyone living today will no doubt find useful.

DIFFERENT MINDSETS

It is common to learn in history, especially in Western philosophy, that humans are naturally selfish and governed by self-interest. The English philosopher Thomas Hobbes said in his work *Leviathan*, which discusses the concept that, of the 'voluntary acts of every man, the object is some good to himself'. While the founder of psychoanalysis Sigmund Freud went further to say in his book *Civilization and Its Discontents* that civilisation is a 'human achievement that stands in opposition to human nature, [where] humans are inherently unhappy as they are forced to surrender their true instinctual/selfish nature under the oppressive but necessary civilizing forces'.

There has been some pushback against this idea that people are bad. In his book *Human kind: A Hopeful History*, Rutger Bregman examined the historic claims that led to this assumption and actually came to the conclusion that 'it is realistic, as well as revolutionary to assume that people are good'. Bregman is one of a number of Western thinkers who have mooted the idea that humans are intrinsically good. These include Jean-Jacques Rousseau, who influenced the progress of the Enlightenment throughout Europe with his political theory on 'General will' and believed that 'one man by nature is just as good as any other, [and] a man could be just without virtue and good without effort'.

25

However, this optimistic view of humanity has just not taken hold in quite the same way.

Western psychology tends to be divided into two schools of thought:

- psychological egoism – our motivation is always perceived to be in our own self-interest;
- psychological altruism – it is possible to have truly selfless motives.

But in Eastern thought, especially that which can be traced back to Confucianism (and Daoism and Buddhism), the two are not laid out as opposites. There is a deeper understanding that selfish actions can have altruistic motives and altruistic actions can have selfish motives – the importance lies in being aware of our actions and motives.

In Eastern thought, balance and harmony are the tenets of rationality, which differs from the Western concept of rationality considered to have come from Greek mythology. In Greek culture, binaries such as man/god, eternal/mortal, good/bad are characteristic, and it is assumed that this is the root in Western thought, while China developed its own ideas of reason earlier, not founded in opposites, but in balance and harmony.

This balance is important to Rén. In Rén, through a philosophy based on our relationship with the world around us, we can achieve perfection not by focusing on altruism and altruistic action, but through accepting that perfectionism is a journey and not a goal. Confucius himself loved learning and championed the benefits of lifelong learning. He believed that life was a 'mandate from heaven', which meant that living in the 'right' way – responsible, resolute and Rén – was extremely important to him. For Confucius, learning is the vital responsibility decreed from on high – our natural duty, from which he developed his teachings on Rén.

Confucius saw that social and political connections are not opposites, but interconnected (politics being the control of power through position or status, which differs depending on the relationship and circumstances). It is the achievement of balance in our socio-political relationships that is core to Rén and built on the faith that Confucius had in humanity's goodness. He saw that humans are naturally good and would instinctively want to do the right thing in all situation, hindered only by a lack of knowledge and understanding. His teachings were created to guide us towards achieving Rén, to make the journey easier, understanding that at the core of all of us is good.

> Being dependable, determined, humble and cautious in speech, brings one closer to Rén.
>
> THE ANALECTS 13.27

As humans have traversed what might seem to have been a long evolutionary period, the last century or so has pulled us through an extremely fast-paced period of change, from the Industrial Revolution that forced us to adapt to new ways of life quickly, to the recent pandemic that has tested us in ways we couldn't even imagine before. This constant progress drags us along in its tide, denying us the space and time to consider what is happening around us. With a lack of guidance, we often feel out of our depth, just struggling to survive and keep up. This distracts us from grounding ourselves in our daily practices, which increases with the pace of progress in our technological world.

Within this fast pace of change, Rén is even more important in providing clarity to our thinking and guidance to our actions. Moving away from philosophy that insists on framing the world as a series of polar opposites, practising Rén will allow us to approach the diverse issues in life with a sense of balance and harmony, using kind and compassionate actions.

AUTHOR'S NOTE

Here, it is important to note that during Confucius's time, the structure and anxieties of society were different and that influenced some of Confucius's teachings. Formal education was only available to those who wanted to pursue a career in governance, and those roles were heavily influenced by concepts of ethics. Due to this, Confucius spent quite a lot of time on issues of governance. There are also problematic references to gender in his text that were typical of his time and have been compounded in the translation process across different eras. For the purposes of this book, I have chosen not to include most of the political teachings of Confucius as they are not relevant to learning Rén for our personal development and fulfilment. When it comes to the more problematic references to gender and diversity that have evolved over the last two centuries, I have chosen to reframe Confucius's teachings so that they may be understood universally and our focus can be placed on the core value of his teachings rather than the socio-political issues of his time. For example, jūn zǐ 君子 is often used in ancient China to refer to someone who is learned, like a sage. However, in translation, it is repeatedly referred to as a 'gentleman' or 'nobleman', which distorts the meaning of the teachings to encompass gender and class. In this case, I have replaced the reference in the translation to 'the

learned' instead. In *The Analects*, Confucius often referred to jūn zǐ as someone who is practising to become Rén.

THIS BOOK

Part One: Rén and You

Part Two: Rén and Family and Friends

Part Three: Rén, Society and the Wider World

Part Four: Rén Today

Using Confucius's lessons, stories and exercises, together we will explore how the basic principles of Rén can help us connect better with family, friends and colleagues and how they will give us tools to become helpful members of society and find fulfilment in ideas of community, justice, morality and compassion.

I encourage you to read this book at a pace that is comfortable to you. Feel free to scribble, fold and mark the pages that are important to you, so you can revisit them again later. Even after you've finished reading, from time to time go back to specific sections to jog your memory and be reminded of your Rén journey. I hope this book will be your companion through a lifelong study and will bring you more and more moments of calm, fulfilment and happiness.

PART
ONE

RÉN
AND YOU

TAKING CARE
OF OURSELVES

I was not born with knowledge, but being fond
of what is simple and old, I love to learn.

THE ANALECTS 7:20

IN EVERYTHING WE DO, the choice always begins
with us. There are many who might say that they just
follow the tide, allowing life to sweep them away and
go from one moment to the next organically. Though it
would be easy to assume we can take a passive role, this isn't
so. Whether we allow a moment to pull us along or try to
resist, they are in essence both active choices and it is in this
recognition or awareness of the choices we make that our
work on Rén begins. Confucius taught that learning is the
foundation to Rén and in this first part of the book, Rén
and You, that is where we will start.

SELF-AWARENESS

Rén is within reach when we learn
extensively, deepen our resolve, question
in detail and reflect on issues.

THE ANALECTS 19:6

How well do we know ourselves? Do we often engage with our own thoughts and ideas, or do we ignore them? Do we know ourselves well enough to predict what we will say or do next, or how we will react to certain situations? At first glance these might seem like foolish questions, or we might assume that we must already know ourselves, but in our fast-paced lives, we don't usually spend time learning about and reflecting on ourselves.

In Confucius's teachings, he promotes an engagement with learning. In our modern lives, we're often told to 'slow down' or 'take time' in contrast to the 'fast-paced' development around us and this can create anxiety when already we might feel over stretched by our existing lifestyles. Where are we going to find the opportunity to slow down and where is there extra time for us to 'take'?

In order to better understand how we learn, we need to dig into our idea of 'learning'. When I think about learning,

I see myself at my old school, at a single blue plastic table in a large, light classroom with cement flooring and chalk dust permanently in the air – a memory from childhood. In school, the purpose of study always seemed clear and the books and stationery that I had on my desk or in my bag were always enough for the task at hand. Somehow, it felt simpler then. I can see myself leaning over the desk, open book and pencil in hand, concentrating on a task. I find learning about myself to be about imagining or recalling specific moments in my life, then analysing them to understand their details and importance.

By engaging in the above exercise, I'm better able to understand what I assume to be learning. My experience brought me to a childhood memory that I've clearly labelled as a moment of 'learning'. Having worked for over 20 years, I'm surprised that the chosen memory was from school and not a more recent experience. This trinket of information gives me a new self-awareness and also forms a new understanding of what my mind sees 'learning' to be, creating further recognition of my own habits. For example, when I feel overwhelmed by work, it is helpful for me just to sit down with a notepad and a pen and write out a full list of what I'm working on. This process mimics that memory of learning and it sets me up, physically and mentally, to concentrate and engage only with the task at hand. It brings clarity in moments of anxiety. After such sessions, I feel calmer and more in control of the tasks I have.

ACTIVITY
LEARNING

To help you begin to find ways of understanding yourself, try taking a moment, closing your eyes and imagining yourself 'learning'. What image comes to mind? Is it a memory, or a made-up situation?

Perhaps you're at a library or listening to a teacher speak. What objects do you have around you and what position are you in – sitting, standing, lying down? Fill in as much detail as you can before moving on.

Now, think of a recent moment that feels similar, where you were perhaps in the same physical position or at the same place. You might have been alone at home in the quiet (like at a library) or watching a colleague's presentation at work. What were you doing? How did you feel? Is there a connection between the imagined moment and the recent moment?

Take time to explore and try to find out what your ideal learning environment is. It might take a few tries before you discover something more about yourself through the exercise, or find out what your ideal learning environment is like. Or you might find that your response changes depending on what kind of learning activities you are doing or imagining. This will be different for everyone and that's okay. The process itself – of engaging with our imagination and memory, and analysing those moments – is more important in our journey into self-awareness than the results.

SELF-CULTIVATION

> The learned focus their attention in nine
> ways: clarity in vision; acuity in hearing;
> gentle in expressions; respectful in conduct;
> sincere in speech; conscientious in actions;
> when in doubt, they seek answers; when
> angry, they are aware of consequences; and
> when there are opportunities, they consider
> what is appropriate.

THE ANALECTS 16:10

Confucius's teachings reflect mindfulness techniques through asserting 'respectful attention' and 'self-cultivation'. In the above quote, he asks for attentiveness and focus in our daily habits. This is part of our self-learning. When we begin to be aware of our actions, we begin to exercise mindfulness in our lives. There are many approaches on how to practise mindfulness, from meditation to yoga, apps to classes. Our paths to developing mindful practices will vary depending on our own personality and what is effective for us.

I have found two main types of meditation that have helped me: contemplative and integrated. As these are commonly practised, I hope they will be fruitful for you too.

CONTEMPLATIVE MEDITATION is also known as mindfulness meditation. It is usually practised at the start or the end of the day, or when we're able to allocate time to being still during the day – for example, during a commute or on our lunch break. Contemplative meditation helps clear our minds. There are different approaches to this – using audio guides, or gazing at a candle, or lying or sitting in complete darkness – and it will often involve a focus on our breathing or thoughts. In this practice, any thoughts that come through our minds will be acknowledged and let go, as we work towards clearing our heads for a moment of calm and clarity.

INTEGRATED MEDITATION is a term that I give to meditation that can be practised at any point of the day during an activity or action. It is done by imagining that we are hovering over and looking down at ourselves as we go about our activities. This is an out-of-body simulation, as if we are watching through a camera positioned just on top of our shoulders, while we direct all our actions at ourselves: walk, talk, drink, stop, smile, etc. This separation provides a buffer for us to observe ourselves without judgement: to just watch, take note and move on.

Through practising both types of meditation, I began to find it easier to be more attentive to my senses and my actions, especially during more difficult situations. I also started to understand my reactions and actions better.

ACTIVITY
MINDFULNESS PRACTICE

Experiment with different mindfulness practices that you feel will improve your focus on your own actions and reactions. When you find something that suits you, create a routine. If you already have a mindfulness routine, don't change it, but try the following activity anyway. A change in practice might unlock new self-awareness. When you feel comfortable, make notes after your contemplative practice. Allocate a different focus, each time thinking about events over the last few days. Here are some examples:

- How observant have you been of the environment or people around you?
- When you were in a conversation, how well were you paying attention to the details?
- When you were eating, how much thought did you have about the taste and smell of the food?
- Did you have any experiences that reminded you of a memory? What were they?
- Were you aware of your facial expressions and posture during the day?

As you get more comfortable recalling and noting the experiences, try to bring in more moments of reflection throughout the day, perhaps using the integrated meditation practice above.

Check in with yourself occasionally to consider how your personal mindfulness practice has developed and contemplate whether this has brought any changes to your life and how you manage it. You might find yourself being hyperaware, questioning your actions before you make them, or you might feel that though your practice feels natural and is blended into your daily life, you're not sure what benefits it brings yet. Whatever conclusions you might draw, remember that this is a journey that takes time and this specific activity is just to observe. Be kind and gentle with yourself.

ISOLATION AND SELF-CRITICISM

> Those who truly love to learn evaluates daily
> what they have yet to understand and reviews
> what they have mastered monthly so they will
> not forget.

THE ANALECTS 19:5

A quick way to embrace self-awareness is through isolation. Most mindfulness practice requires an isolated environment anyway, because it promotes self-reflection. When we are alone and without distractions for a longer period of time, we create opportunities to self-reflect as our mind wanders. If we approach it conscientiously, we can develop a mindfulness practice. However, moments of accidental awareness, perhaps triggered by forced isolation or harsh criticisms, could easily agitate us.

During the recent pandemic, we had to endure prolonged periods of isolation, where some of us went through lockdown alone, with a partner and/or our family, or with friends or flatmates (the combinations are plenty). Whatever situation we were in, many of us found ourselves using the same space throughout the day for all our activities – work, rest, entertainment, meals, and more. This confinement and repetition created an environment of isolation that unsettled many of us because we were not accustomed to living with ourselves. The lack of social events meant that we didn't have the ability or the opportunity to distract ourselves, that we were left with just ourselves and were forced to get to know ourselves better. Similarly, looking inward – for those of us who are not used to it – might create stress and anxiety.

The teaching from Confucius at the beginning of this section highlights how this inward learning can be positive. A person who loves to learn would assess themselves daily to analyse what they do not know and continue to practise and grow what they know. If we do not love learning about ourselves (yet) or are not prepared to do so (yet), then when we learn a fact about ourselves, we might become obsessed with it.

As a teenager, I didn't notice that I chewed with my mouth open until a close friend pointed it out. After that, I could no longer chew without feeling self-conscious as I was now hyperaware. To this day, I still notice when others do it. This example had an 'easy fix' in that I stopped chewing with my mouth open, but I also had to learn to tolerate it when others do so.

Sometimes, we might find out details about ourselves that we find unbelievable, even faults that seem to go against our personal principles or moral stance. If there was a situation where someone called out our behaviour as racist, sexist, inconsiderate or thoughtless, we would be hurt, because we would never imagine ourselves to be those things. We might even react defensively in the situation. This is why it is important for us to root our study of Rén in learning. When we accept that we are constantly in a state of learning, it allows us to better receive criticism, especially from ourselves, which will then allow us to grow and improve. Because Rén requires self-awareness and self-honesty, in our practice, we will find ourselves in vulnerable positions of self-criticism that we might be unused to. Like watching ourselves in a video recording, where we start to pick at every gesture, posture and movement and cringe at the sound of our own voice, Rén involves looking hard at ourselves.

Following Confucius's teaching, we need to be honest with our own criticism about what we need to learn and also continue to practise and improve on what we have already learnt. Though it helps to be direct, this shouldn't be harsh – remember, improving ourselves is an act of kindness. The pace at which we do this will differ individually, but at least we can take comfort in the knowledge that all of us who are practising to be Rén are doing this together.

SELF-CARE

> When we become kinder to ourselves, we can
> be kinder to the world.

HAEMIN SUNIM
*Love for Imperfect Things: How to Accept Yourself in a
World Striving for Perfection*

In air travel, we're always reminded to sort our own life vest or an oxygen mask first. This is because if we were incapacitated, we would not be in position to help others in our care, so really, we need to help ourselves first before helping others. In Rén, everything we do starts with us, as individuals, and this includes self-care: we need to know that we are starting from a strong, healthy position in order to help others.

Confucius taught that being Rén depends on no one but ourselves and so we need to start with being kind and compassionate to ourselves. In mindfulness practice, we need to get to know our body and mind well, to be able to identify if we're in a healthy and comfortable state. And if we are not, it's important that we give ourselves permission to seek help when we need it.

ACTIVITY
SELF-CARE

Before you begin your mindfulness practices, check in with yourself by asking the following questions:

- As far as I know, am I healthy in body and mind?
- Am I comfortable in body and mind?
- Am I comfortable with my surroundings? The spaces and people?
- Is there any unease within myself?

Whatever the answers may be, try exploring the questions further by asking yourself why you answered as such. If your answers do not require any action, just acknowledge them without judgement and continue with your practice.

If there are negative responses that appear frequently, or demonstrate growing anxiety or unease, give yourself permission to seek help and support. If things are difficult, we need to try and get help from a professional. Talking to someone you trust might help you process smaller issues. Understand that seeking help isn't limited to physical ailments and that applying self-care is an important aspect of Rén. The key to this activity is to get to know yourself better, so be honest.

BEING INDEPENDENT

Being Rén depends on no one but yourself.

THE ANALECTS 12:1

When we're committed to studying and practising to become Rén, it's important to understand that if we feel incapacitated in any way, we need to improve our own wellbeing and health first before trying to proceed with our practice as it might create more harm otherwise.

Consider a broken watch. No matter how much we polish the watch or change its straps or battery, if we do not look into the problem and mend it, it will not function as a watch. It might look good as an accessory, but it is without all its functionality. If we are incapacitated and we force ourselves to practise to be Rén without exploring our own health issues, we will just be adding cosmetic changes that might feel good for a while, but will not last.

EMOTIONAL BY NATURE

> In nature we are similar, but our habits
> separate us.

THE ANALECTS 17:2

In all situations, good and bad, our first reactions tend to be emotional ones. This is most obvious in children. If you watch their reactions, you'll likely find that their responses are purely emotional. They will cry when sad, throw tantrums when frustrated and laugh when they are having fun. They also tend to cry when they are tired, unable to do anymore. This is the case for children from any part of the world, especially babies. As humans, we are emotional by nature and in this way, as Confucius suggests in the quote above, we are similar, regardless of where we are from.

Have you ever wished you could act like a child at times? When I have too much on, I find myself wanting to be alone and just cry, yet fighting the urge for some reason. I often ask myself: why is it so bad to cry? Why, as a society, do we characterise crying as weak and helpless? As adults, we have learned that impulse control is a sign of maturity and we have been trained to stop emoting or reacting immediately to situations. We learn how to take 'considered approaches' or give it that split second to check if our reactions are appropriate. The need for impulse control does not mean that our emotional responses are wrong or unimportant, it just helps us to manage ourselves as a society in a more considerate way. It helps reduce dramatic outbursts or unnecessary disagreements caused by emotional reactions.

In nature, our emotions are how we naturally react to situations to help us survive, and because the concept of survival has changed so drastically for humans over the last few millennia, our emotions and how we process them have changed too. Naturally, this varies according to the customs of different societies throughout the world. In Confucius's quote above, he notes this as a development through our habits.

Take pain, for example: when we hurt ourselves, we cry. Through science and research, we know now that crying is a naturally self-soothing mechanism. When we cry, physiologically, we release opioids (substances that produce morphine-like effects) that help numb pain, which increases our pain threshold for the moment we are suffering, and we also release oxytocin, a calming hormone that reassures us. Because crying is often seen by society as a sign of weakness, over time we've developed other ways to manage pain through new habits. Shouting and swearing is one, an effective method as it has been found that when we shout and swear, our pain threshold increases and our pain awareness reduces.

Being kind also has its soothing mechanisms. When we engage in acts of kindness, it boosts the release of oxytocin (the love hormone that promotes human connection), dopamine (a chemical messenger for pleasure) and serotonin (the mood stabiliser for feelings of wellbeing and happiness). This has also changed through time, through new habits, especially in more recent years with technology and social media popularity. Successful social interactions – for example, when someone likes your posts on social media – triggers a release of dopamine in our system and social media algorithms play on this.

When we are used to getting hits of pleasure through dopamine, when it is taken away, our brain cues us to participate more for more positive outcomes. This creates something similar to smoking and gambling addictions, where if we perceive a reward (dopamine) to be delivered at random (when someone likes our post), and if checking for the reward comes at little cost, we end up checking habitually. Even when we are not looking at our smartphones, the notification sounds are enough to give us a hit of dopamine, inviting us to look at our social media accounts. This becomes a distraction from actual real-life experiences that would be more fulfilling.

The changes that we see in our habits, in how we deal with pain or how we find new sources of pleasure, show how humans' emotional responses have been affected by social pressures and technological developments. The effects, in turn, have caused new habits (good and bad) to be adapted over time. Confucius taught that humans are alike by nature and that our habits – what we do – separate or differentiate us. Our initial emotional response is our natural expression of how we really feel about something and if we did not develop customs and etiquette our societies and lifestyles we would probably find our emotional responses to similar throughout the world.

If we consider Confucius's teaching, which requires us to focus on our self-awareness and learn to understand our own emotional responses, we can gain an insight into the emotional habits that have developed within us.

ACTIVITY
EMOTIONAL HABITS

Are you aware of some of your habits? Consider whether they are linked to an emotional/hormonal pay-off. When you find yourself practising these habits, pay attention to your body and mind's reactions. If you stop practising the habits, how do you feel?

If your emotional habits are affecting your physical or mental health, or if you would like to overcome an addiction, please consider seeking professional help.

EMBRACING EMOTIONS

In mourning, we grieve so we may then stop.

THE ANALECTS 19:14

In Confucius's teachings, a good habit is to allow ourselves to engage with an emotion, exhaust it and move on. Often, when we manage our emotions, we also tend to bottle them up. Mindfulness practice can help release these emotions through time, but allowing ourselves proper engagement in the experience is more important. In Confucius's teachings, the mourning ritual is often used to reflect this as it is one of the rituals that Confucius most respects.

When we give ourselves permission to engage with an emotion fully, as a crude analogy, it is as if we have completed a task on a checklist. Imagine that you have accumulated emotions through the days, weeks or even months, and the checklist becomes too big to track or make sense of. When this happens, it creates a cascade of emotions whose causes we may be unable to identify and which may overwhelm us at any time.

When we experience positive emotions like joy, happiness or triumph, we usually allow ourselves to fully engage with the emotion until the feeling is spent. This is because our body relishes the hormones that are released, which naturally allow us to relax into the experience.

When we experience negative or difficult emotions like fear, our body releases adrenaline and cortisol, which increases our energy levels for a fight or flight response in a dangerous situation. In modern lifestyles, the build-up of stress (and a lack of physical danger) creates a different type of fear, which still triggers the release of the same hormones. Even without the physical threat, adrenaline and cortisol trigger anxiety in the body.

As anger, fear, grief and other negative emotions evoke harsh internal reactions, we manage and control these more frequently. Confucius reminds us that first and foremost, we need to consider the consequences of our actions in these situations. Once that is managed, when we have a moment after to reflect, we should allow ourselves to replay and analyse the emotions that have accumulated. We will all have different methods to deal with such situations. In the past, I have found myself screaming into or hitting a pillow, crying or swearing, and though these allow for a physical release, the issues were not resolved. In the end, I learnt that it takes being focused and calm to fully consider the experience, understand it, find a solution or action for it, if necessary – and then move on.

ACTIVITY
EMOTIONAL RESPONSES

During your day, check in on yourself often and ask, 'What am I feeling right now?' and 'Has anything brought it on?' Write down your emotions and reasons. At the end of the day, review your list and try to remember what you were doing – your actions and reactions. Do you have any thoughts on them? Were they expected? Are there any residual emotions on an unresolved issue?

If there are, spend time engaging with the problem to consider an appropriate action, if necessary – setting out a plan will begin to appease your emotional needs. When you think of the issue again, pay attention to how you feel – your original emotions should be spent and you might have new ones attached to the issue depending on how it is resolved. Sometimes, when we have accumulated emotions within us, the trigger to an emotional reaction or outburst might not actually reveal its root cause. Through being more self-aware, we can avoid these situations which may cause misunderstandings and create unnecessary unease.

IMPROVING WITH KINDNESS

The learned is free from worries and fears.
If our conscience is clear, what have we to
worry about or fear?

THE ANALECTS 12:4

Confucius was realistic about human nature and understood that we are not infallible. Mistakes are expected, but he taught that they only remain as mistakes if they are left uncorrected and nothing is done about them.

In this section, where we learn about Rén and ourselves, we need to apply this lesson on correcting mistakes to how we manage ourselves. When we spot an issue in ourselves or learn something uncomfortable about ourselves, it's important to explore the issue to discern if it requires attention and if there needs to be a change or correction put in place. But before we do so, we need to understand that Confucius isn't teaching us to be critical of ourselves to make us feel bad, he is asking us to be critical of ourselves to find areas for improvement, spaces for growth. He sees that if we are able to improve ourselves in this way, there won't be anything that causes us worry, fear or anxiety. In Rén, knowing that when we face the errors of our ways with resolution to change, and we learn from the experience, we can have a clear conscience that we have done our best and can continue to do better.

I have a friend and colleague who I feel embraces this fully in her life. She is an inspiration for much of this book. When I got to know her, I was blown away by the clarity she had in how she managed herself. She addressed her worries and anxieties with action. When she received criticisms, she examined those criticisms with as much objectivity as she could muster in order to clearly consider if and how she had erred, then she would work out how she could improve and evolve. Like everyone, she has human emotions, and so honest self-reflection is not so easy as I make it sound. However, being focused and processing these difficult emotions systematically means that she is able to treat herself kindly. This allows her to move on more quickly and effectively, knowing that any errors have been faced with honesty. As a result, her conscience is clear.

Often, when we talk about being kind to ourselves, we automatically think about treats – things like favourite foods, massages, shopping trips and holiday. How we manage when we get hurt, fall ill, or tackle difficult emotions can also be an act of kindness to ourselves. If someone else got hurt, an act of kindness would be to help them get treatment to ease the pain. If we get hurt or fall ill, we see a doctor to ease our suffering. Because we are aware that time is necessary for healing, we can look forward to our recovery as the end goal, to help us through the period of treatment, which might be long or arduous. The treatment is part of how we can be kind to ourselves.

This is similar in moments of turbulent emotions. When we use our mindfulness practice to reflect on criticisms of ourselves, we need to do so without judgement and be gentle with ourselves. As we grow comfortable with ourselves, we can start to pay attention to areas that might need improvement or 'treatment'. A mental health issue or an emotional difficulty should be treated just like a physical injury, as an act of kindness to ourselves. Confucius taught that it is the responsibility of someone who is Rén to change and improve, and it is through kindness that we do so, in order that we continue to do good.

ACTIVITY
APPLYING KINDNESS TO LEARNING

Do you have worries, fears or anxieties? Is there a particular concern that keeps haunting your thoughts? Note it down and ask yourself if you are taking any action to address it. If not, try to find out why.

Try not to judge yourself during this process. Rather, encourage yourself to imagine a time in the future where you might not have this worry anymore and how that might feel. Even if it might seem an impossibility, remind yourself that it is your responsibility to be kind to yourself and improving your health (both physically and mentally) is part of this process.

Take small steps to correct this issue and if the task seems too daunting, try telling someone about it. Being able to describe the issue is a step closer to learning how to correct it. And if necessary, seek professional help.

Remember, to be Rén, our practice itself is the process and as long as we are learning and improving – whether in a big or small way – we are on the right track because we are practising self-care and being kind to ourselves.

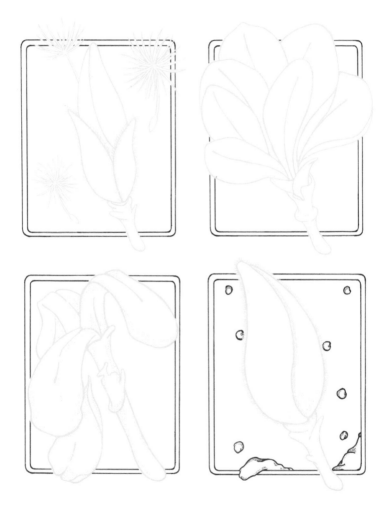

REWARDS AND CHANGE

> Rén without learning leads to ignorance.
> Knowledge without learning leads to
> disruption. Loyalty without learning leads
> to hurt. Honesty without learning leads to
> intolerance. Courage without learning leads
> to chaos. Devotion without learning leads
> to recklessness.
>
> THE ANALECTS 17:8

When we nurture children from a young age, we naturally praise them as they learn daily tasks that equip them for life. These could be when they eat well, brush their teeth, wash their hands or tidy up after themselves. These habits form the basis of a healthy person so when we see them children performing them, we say, 'Well done,' or we give them a sticker.

As adults, we could benefit from treating ourselves as we would children. When we complete the basic tasks that are expected of an independent adult – actions of self-care such as taking a shower, flossing our teeth, cooking our meals, not eating junk food – we should take time to acknowledge a job well done. We need to give ourselves praise to encourage habits of self-care going forward. What we will find when we do so is that we will start to be more aware of our actions and take more responsibility for what we choose to do for ourselves. The things that we praise ourselves for will change over time to those that are more complex: well done for not getting angry, well done for taking the other person's criticism into consideration, well done for saying no to taking on more work/social events that will damage your health. This habit allows us to increase our self-awareness and learning in a gentle way. Using acts of kindness on ourselves will help us develop a habit of self-care that can slowly expand to support more complicated situations.

I'm not a morning person and I will be the first to admit that I am grumpiest when I first wake up. Since becoming a mother though, I have found that I do not have the luxury of being grumpy in the mornings, for my mood determines my daughter's. If I woke up grumpy and was unsmiling and short with her, I would immediately receive the same treatment. However, because she is a toddler, it would be many times more exaggerated. And the consequences of this? Well, it would be very difficult to get her ready for the day or encourage her to go to nursery. I quickly learnt this after a few failed attempts to get her ready to leave the house. It helps that it is easy to want to smile and hug my daughter first thing in the morning, but it is still something that I had to change about myself and that I discovered through experience. I would have laughed at anyone who told me when I was younger that it was possible for me to wake up early with a smile and get on with my day immediately without coffee first. Nowadays, I only have my first coffee after my daughter is at nursery, when I'm ready to sit down at my desk to work.

What this experience demonstrated to me was that our own personalities or habits aren't actually fixed. What we are willing to change about ourselves depends on what is at stake for us. In the example above, what was at stake was my personal sanity and my family's peace. I was able to maintain my morning grumpiness when it was just my husband because I didn't see why I should change my morning coffee routine. As a couple who know each other well, we probably compromised in this situation, but I also got away with being inconsiderate because he is an adult, who could manage not to engage with me until I had had that coffee. Though aware of my morning grumpiness, I wasn't aware or considerate about how that might have affected my husband at the time, or my parents and sister before. It took a toddler to show me how selfish my own actions were and more importantly, how tolerant others are, even if we're unaware of it. In this way, though I believed I was loving and loyal to my family, my inability to reflect on my behaviour meant that I had caused harm to them. As Confucius notes, this is why it is important to keep an open mind through learning.

ACTIVITY
CHANGING HABITS

Think about the various habits that you have. Have you recently changed any of them? If so, why did you do so? What was the incentive?

Do you have a habit that you would like to change? What's at stake? If you feel that this is a difficult habit to change, can you raise the stakes or increase the reward?

BEING ATTENTIVE TO OURSELVES

> The learned's journey is long, as it ends only
> in death; and their burden is heavy, as their
> duty is to be Rén.

THE ANALECTS 8:7

Confucius taught that we can achieve Rén by learning broadly and deepening our resolution in life. In our practice, he insisted that it always begins with ourselves, suggesting we question closely and reflect on things near at hand for focus and self-awareness.

As dedication to becoming Rén is a lifelong journey, it is important that the foundation of our learning is strong. Developing a good understanding of ourselves through mindfulness establishes this. When we find that we are attentive to ourselves more naturally, we need to be kind to ourselves and practise self-care and self-development. Through awareness, we will learn more about what drives us and how we can better adapt to change. Using these techniques, we can build a good foundation for Rén.

UNDERSTANDING BEING HUMAN

Follow the Dào, stand on virtue, depend on Rén and enjoy in the arts.

THE ANALECTS 7:6

ONFUCIUS'S PHILOSOPHY OF **Rén** is built around the relationships we have with our communities and environment around us. In studying to be Rén, we must accept that we are social beings by nature. Our personalities might be introverted or extroverted, quiet or outgoing, but by nature, we understand through Rén that we require social interactions to live and to flourish.

SOCIAL BEINGS

> The learned acts in harmony but does not
> imitate, the petty-minded imitates but does
> not act in harmony.

THE ANALECTS 13:23

Confucius saw the value of harmony in communities. He taught that our actions have consequences: what we do affects others and we need to be aware of that.

Recently, my four-year-old daughter started getting interested in speaking to new people. She began by asking me to tell people I'm talking to (such as friends and shop staff) her name and after a few times, I suggested she tell them directly and she got excited about this. Like many children, she has been taught by her teachers and parents, the dangers of being with strangers. So, she would wait for me to interact with someone first, or she would ask me if it was ok before doing so.

When we were at the bookshop, as I exchanged pleasantries at the till, she went up to the bookseller and said, 'Hello, my name is Aoife.' In the midst of the quiet and professional exchange I was having with him, he looked up at her, broke into a big smile and said, 'Hello,

I'm Mark. Nice to meet you.' Mark continued chatting with my daughter while he rang up the books and took my payment, and we all parted with huge smiles on all our faces. When we went to the café, she did the same thing again and made friends with Antony, the barista. Her actions proved disarming, warming up what would usually be quite functional, unexceptional exchanges.

Out of curiosity, my daughter had stumbled on the fact that successful interactions with people gave her a buzz. As she chatted with them, her body produced dopamine and she felt the pleasure. Although this was the first time she learnt that she enjoyed these exchanges, it wasn't the first time she had affected someone else. Even as a baby, there were occasions when she would catch the eye of a waitress or a passer-by and they would smile back at her. We've had people come up to us and tell us that she has made their day, just by smiling at them or being cute. These small exchanges can be very uplifting.

In one of my past jobs, I remember working for someone who was known for their bad and unpredictable temper. Daily, we would go up to their assistant and ask, 'What's the weather?' before deciding whether it was a good time to approach them or not. In another job, I was taught on the first day that I had to compile a list of all the things I needed to talk to the boss about and just maintain that list until he was ready or had time for me. Needless to say, I didn't last long in either of those roles as I felt shackled and in a constant state of anxiety. For me, the price I had to pay to navigate difficult personalities was to make adjustments to myself and that wasn't worth it for the experience I was gaining in those roles. I have learnt through various jobs that managers who played nurturing and aspiring roles suited me best and working with them, I was able to present the best version of myself. This is my personal experience, but likely one that resonates with many people – that positive reinforcement and self-confidence leads to better performance.

As highlighted in Confucius's teachings, these examples showed me how we are constantly being affected by others and have the power to influence others through our actions. Confucius taught that to be Rén, we need to use this awareness to promote a harmonious environment. Where there is harmony, people are more congenial and this creates more fertile conditions for learning, exchange of ideas and collaboration.

ACTIVITY
SMILING AT STRANGERS

Pick a day when you are out and about and try to smile at everyone you pass. At the end of the day, check in on how you feel. Consider whether you have affected someone else's day.

I know how awkward this activity can be if you're not used to connecting with strangers. I do this often and responses vary, with most people returning an awkward smile. Depending on where you are (big city, countryside, at home, on holiday, etc.) you might get different reactions too. However, it never fails to lift my spirits.

UNDERSTANDING OURSELVES THROUGH THE PEOPLE AROUND US

The learned makes friends through their learning and looks to friends for support in Rén.

THE ANALECTS 12:24

Our behaviour, whether consciously or unconsciously, attracts the friends we have. This means that our friends and communities reflect who we are. When we are in our practice to become Rén, we can look at those closest to us and explore how we feel when we are around them and what we think about them in order to gain insights into ourselves.

Looking at the array of friends who have come into my life at different times, I can see the different parts of me that they mirror. There are the friends who were colleagues, friends with a similar life history (who, like me, had moved from Malaysia to the UK), friends I met because our children are the same age, and others. When I consider Confucius's teaching, I begin to see that each of my friends reflects what is important in my life at each moment.

An example that springs to mind is one friend who I met recently. We were introduced by a mutual friend – who was aware of our overlapping interests – over a video call during the pandemic as the UK started its lockdown in March 2020. For more than a year, we didn't have the chance to meet in real life, but our friendship flourished as we met up online often to collaborate on projects or just catch up about life. If I think about her personality and consider all the values that I believe are important to her, I would reflect that (because I enjoyed spending time with her) during the time when we met, philosophy, ethics and relationships were important to me.

In the same way, there are relationships that I did not enjoy, with people whom I would refer to as my acquaintances. Those relationships also reflect what was unimportant to me, or what I was at odds with during those times. Such relationships fade over time, having existed only because of a specific situation that had brought us together – after which, there seemed to be nothing to hold the relationship together.

Through personal experience, I've found that friendships that continue to develop through different phases of life and that are grounded in a variety of issues that are important to me are the strongest – they are friends who remain close. This might resonate with many who have found that long relationships, as in a family or with a partner, that are sustained through a multitude of circumstances eventually develop stronger bonds. As Rén 仁 represents, our individual identities are formed by our engagement with the world we are in, just as we influence the identities of others.

ACTIVITY

REFLECTING ON OUR FRIENDS

Think of your closest friends and consider their priorities in life. How does this reflect your own priorities? By paying more attention to your friends, can you understand yourself better?

ASPIRE, NOT DESIRE

> Do not worry about being unappreciated.
> Rather, aspire to be worthy of appreciation.

THE ANALECTS 4:14

What Confucius is drawing our attention to here is the difference between aspiration and desire. To become Rén, and thus to find fulfilment within ourselves, we must learn how to separate our desires from things we can control. This is all part of cultivating and improving ourselves.

Like the quote above, if we desire a promotion at work, our focus is placed on wanting something that someone else – our manager or boss – has to give us, which is beyond our control. However, if we aspire to be worthy of a promotion, it is something that we can control by working on ways we might improve and be better at our jobs.

An example of this from our daily lives could be when we share our living spaces with others. We might desire a clean and tidy flat and this might seem reasonable. However, if we are sharing the space with someone else, this becomes something that is out of our control (Confucius promotes influencing others through action, not coercion, something we will explore in later sections of this book). In this case, we should change that desire to an aspiration, such as: I want to be tidier, I want to be more organised, or I want to develop a habit of keeping the flat clean and tidy. Or, we might even consider: I aspire to provide an orderly environment for my housemates.

Commuting to work throws up similar challenges. When we set out on a drive or to travel on public transport, often we desire an efficient commute: to arrive on time and to have an uneventful trip. However, there are too many elements that are out of our control: bad traffic, accidents, weather, other commuters, etc. To dwell on this desire for a smooth commute, without disruption, could conversely cause anxiety about factors we can't possibly influence. If we listen to Confucius, we should aspire to have a better commute by setting out earlier or outside of peak hours. Travelling earlier or at a different time is something we can manage and control, and could improve our experience and affect the rest of our day positively.

Confucius says that change has to come from within ourselves – through practising self-cultivation – and not from others. By avoiding desiring, things outside our control and seeking aspirations, and focusing on the things that can be improved by our own actions, we will see ourselves grow and live a more peaceful life.

ACTIVITY
CREATING ASPIRATIONS

Write a list of your desires. These can be things that you want or even goals that you would like to achieve. Consider whether they rely on others to be attained. If they do, rewrite them as aspirations instead. Think about aligning them to your self-development as actionable points.

If there are material things that you desire, consider aspirations that will help your financial situation. For example, aspire to learn to cook better (to spend less eating out), aspire to upskill or learn a new skill (so you can seek better-paying jobs) or aspire to improve yourself at work. If you are able to afford material things but want to justify them, you might also consider using them as rewards for positive behaviour (*see also* Rewards and Change, pages 69).

DRIVEN BY DRAMA:
HARMFUL PLEASURES

There are beneficial and harmful pleasures.
Music, rituals, praise of other's virtues and
having worthy friends – these improve you.
Arrogance, idleness and indulgence – these
impair you.

THE ANALECTS 16:5

In the last two millennia, we have progressed a lot: modernisation in many forms, technological development and globalisation have changed our lifestyles around the world. Technology has brought new forms of pleasures now firmly embedded in our daily lives. In Confucius's time, he generalised the concept of beneficial and harmful pleasures in the quote above. What is important to our practice of becoming Rén is that we recognise there are pleasures that are harmful to us.

In my academic research, I've come to learn how technology has shaped society through mass media and drama is the fuel that keeps us interested in the various forms of entertainment and social media. There are studies looking into this phenomenon and scientists have come to hypothesise that emotionally stimulating stories – drama, in a word – trigger a similar neurobiological mechanism in us as we would experience through social bonding. This means that we receive a similar kind of enjoyment and release of hormones watching drama unfold on TV as we do when we interact and bond with real people.

At the core of drama is gossip that often begins through someone's action. Because that action creates an emotional reaction in us – we might like and approve of it, or hate and disapprove of it – it brings drama that feeds our need for human connection. However, gossip is a harmful pleasure because it idles away time and is unhelpful, even hurtful to others. Even though we might crave the feeling of bonding that gossiping imitates, the act itself neither inspires others to do better, nor does it improve ourselves. It is a pointless exercise at best, a dangerous exercise at worst.

During a trip to New York a few years ago, I was surfing channels when I stopped to watch an advertisement for the news. I don't remember the advert verbatim, but I do recall that it had CCTV footage of someone walking into the subway and the voiceover said, 'A man was seen walking into the subway with a gun today. What happens next? Join us at ten tonight to find out more …' I was really surprised to find that a news programme would try and hook viewers in with such clickbait. If I was truly curious about the incident, I would just read up on other news platforms. When a news organisation – which is supposed to provide factual information on current affairs – uses drama to advertise and play with viewers' emotions, it suggests that viewers might not be interested in watching the news. This made me realise the pervasiveness of drama as a tool in the media today.

Like gossip, drama can also be found in provocative content that elicits intense emotional reactions. When something inspires love or hate, it makes us eager to talk about it, either to promote, or to impede and reject it. The media relies on our need to engage through drama, as we do with gossip. In books, TV, film and online platforms, provocative stories manipulate our emotions through drama. For example, if the intention behind a story were to make us feel sad, they would first make us happy. Playing with contrasting emotions creates a bigger emotional payoff. In the same way, if the intention were for us to be angry, they would make us feel safe and content first. This emotional experience is what gets us addicted to consuming modern media and it becomes a harmful pleasure in our lives if left unchecked or consumed excessively.

ACTIVITY
IS IT GOSSIP?

The next time you are attending a social gathering, pay attention to the topics of discussion and how they are told. Is there content (like gossip) that might harm others? Are the most entertaining stories from those who are able to add some drama to the storytelling?

Try telling a story yourself using the contrasting emotions tactic – if you want your friends to laugh, start with something sad so they'll have a bigger reaction.

APPRECIATING THE CALM

Being Rén requires that we reduce the drama in our lives so that we may fully immerse ourselves in our lives and be mindful and ready to engage with our communities. We can do so by refocusing on appreciating the moments that seem calm and neutral.

These might be moments that are easily forgotten as they happen, but when we recall them at a later time, they bring a sense of contentment. These are moments when everything felt in sync, perhaps because our work

was going well, there were no issues in our relationships and all our family and friends were healthy. During those periods, we usually have no conscious engagement with the moments because there was no drama to hook us in. Time seems to flow smoothly and quickly.

Have you ever been asked how your weekend was, and been unable to recall any details of it? We might brush it off and give the excuse that it was just another typical or uneventful weekend. But things being uneventful actually suggests they were good moments in our lives. We would wish someone an uneventful journey when travelling, so why not wish them an uneventful life? Some may say that an uneventful life means one without achievements as well, but I don't believe this to be true.

New parents know this lesson well, as I learnt just after my daughter was born. When I met nurses or other parents with older children at playgroups, I was often advised to enjoy or treasure the baby moments as they fly by. Often, I found this advice ill-timed as I was stressed and anxious trying to cope with being a new mother, managing a baby who only stopped crying or slept when carried, worried about my baby's health at every moment. Where could I find these moments to enjoy and treasure? As time went by, I found myself dishing out the same advice to new parents who were willing to listen. 'I know it's hard, but try,' I would say, as when I did manage to find the moments myself, I enjoyed them greatly. When my daughter slept in my arms, when she laughed and gurgled at my silly faces, when I nursed her as I binged through different TV series, I found seconds and minutes here and there to enjoy the calm and peace and just to take in those moments. It turned out to be the best advice and I have remembered it ever since.

ACTIVITY
APPRECIATING THE CALM

At random times during the day, take a few photos of people and things that you see daily. It might be something you pass on your daily commute, spaces like your bedroom or your office, colleagues, shopkeepers, even selfies.

When you look back at the pictures, remember the calm moments and try to bring yourself back to that state of mind. As you do this more often, try to acknowledge those moments when they're happening during the day to enjoy and appreciate them to the fullest.

UNDERSTANDING WHAT BEING HUMAN MEANS

> The Rén are the first to bear difficulties
> and last to consider rewards.

THE ANALECTS 6:22

As we develop a deeper appreciation for the calm moments in our lives, we can begin to reflect on Confucius's teaching that in being Rén, our objective isn't rewards. It is to achieve a state where we begin to find fulfilment through our experiences of and from our relationship with the world around us. We do so by appreciating harmony and peace, and understanding that happiness and fulfilment are not rewards to be earned (or desired), but states of being that can be achieved through Rén.

When we practise mindfulness, we become more self-aware and we learn to care first for ourselves and understand what drives us. Then, in being kind to ourselves, we ensure that we are fit and healthy in both body and mind. We also work on any issues that may harm us in the long run by constantly seeking to improve ourselves, correcting any errors along the way. We do so in the understanding that we are social beings and that how we feel and act has consequences for our communities and surroundings. And in our practice of mindfulness, we create aspirations – individual ambition for achievements that do not rely on others – to strive to create more calm moments where we are at peace, clear in our conscience, knowing that we are doing our best and continuing to improve day to day. This is all part of how understanding what being human means helps in our journey to becoming Rén.

RECOGNISING AND EMBRACING RÉN

The learned are supportive, encouraging and personable.

THE ANALECTS 13:28

When I was younger, I believed words like 'kindness' and 'compassion' were soft emotions that didn't belong in a successful person's life. To be successful in life, I thought I had to always be tough. I saw success as being rich and this fuelled the thinking that being business-savvy – coy, sneaky and competitive – was how we found fulfilment. This was no doubt part of my youthful ambition to get the house, car and lifestyle that had been advertised to me as desirable. And it shows the naivete of my thinking.

My father suffered a stroke when I was a teenager and my first boss also suffered one while I was working with him. After their treatments, I remember that they both went back to work and life as if nothing had changed. I am sure that to them, there was a lot of change and plenty of additional anxiety and fear, but because I wasn't privy to any of it, I saw only the fact that they toughed it up and got on with life. Back then, I didn't understand the pressures of society around them and I assumed they placed more importance on their work than their health.

This belief was continually reaffirmed as my friends began to climb corporate ladders and started pulling long hours that would become the norm for so many of us. News of illnesses and divorces began to crop up in our lives. It wasn't until I had a break in my career that I started to have more space to realise that much of what I believed to be 'normal and professional' work ethics was actually unhealthy and that human nature is more complicated than it appears on the surface.

That was in the noughties, and I hope that mindsets have now changed and improved through the decades. However, it is only recently that I have come to appreciate Confucius's teaching that being supportive of others and congenial in society is more fulfilling, even in professional circumstances and in business. Studying Rén has taught me that centring a life practice on myself which doesn't rely on others frees my mind from stresses and worries that are beyond my control.

Accepting we cannot and should not change others pulls the focus back within. As we practise being Rén following Confucius's teachings, we can start to think about how we might recognise Rén around us.

LEARNING TO RECOGNISE RÉN

> Those who are virtuous always have teachings to impart, but those who have teachings to impart are not always virtuous. Those who are Rén will always be courageous, but those who are courageous are not always Rén.
>
> THE ANALECTS 14:4

At its core, Rén can be understood as being kind, compassionate, benevolent, moral and loving. Someone who is Rén would also improve themselves through their own positive actions, but do not expect or desire anything from others and do not belittle others. Someone who is Rén is on a permanent journey to develop themselves to be a helpful member of the world and they are able to find fulfilment and happiness in this journey. Knowing all this is useful, but how can we recognise Rén around us?

Growing up in big cities meant that I developed a sense of cynicism towards others around me as a form of survival habit. We learn not to talk to strangers as children, we learn that if someone is following us on the road, they probably have bad intentions, we learn that there is a lot of danger around us and that we should keep vigilant. Wrapped up in this fear, it is hard to let our guard down and to bring ourselves to recognise Rén characteristics that might be around us.

When I think about Rén characteristics, I think about my cat, Chomel. In her day-to-day connection with us, her human family, Chomel managed to create a unique bond with each of us, by showing understanding and compassion. My family had many cats (growing up in Malaysia, I would often rescue strays) and though Chomel was like all the others, she was also special. When she died, we all mourned her for different reasons because we loved her as one of the family.

Chomel and my father had a spiritual connection. During her short years with us, my father had a daily routine of prayers that lasted for over an hour each morning. And every single morning, Chomel would sit by his side and follow his prayers, never disturbing him, just following him in his routine. It was as if she understood what he was doing and was participating in her own way, something even I, as my father's daughter, did not think to do.

As the person in my family responsible for all the stray cats that come and live with us, my father told me after Chomel's death, 'No more.' He couldn't manage another pet in his life and my guess is that he could not bear to replace Chomel, nor could he perceive another cat as having the kind of compassion and understanding that Chomel did.

Though Chomel's actions were not unusual as many pets do show that level of 'human-ness', I recognise her actions as Rén and I remember Chomel with love, because she came across as selfless and considerate: she changed her (cat) behaviours around each of us and our habits as if she understood that it helped us build a loving environment around her, around ourselves – something that I only realised after she left. When we anthropomorphise non-humans in this way, we are able to spot Rén characteristics because they are not the animal characteristics that we are expecting.

Recognising human traits is common to storytelling too. From Disney cartoons to sci-fi movies, to timeless children's stories, we anthropomorphise animals and robots to bring out human values, usually through compassionate action. Do you remember Cinderella's animal friends who helped mend her dress? Or the robot in *Big Hero 6* who sacrifices himself to save the boy? There's also Paddington Bear and Number 5 from *Short Circuit*. Back in ancient Greece, animals were used in Aesop's fables to convey moral stories.

Because we expect humans to have Rén characteristics, and while this might be contradicted by some of us (like me) having learnt to be distrustful of others, we may not realise when we do spot Rén behaviours around us. We can break this chain, or create a new way of seeing Rén around us by being Rén ourselves. When we practise being considerate, kind and compassionate in our own actions, we start to see this behaviour reflected in others, and we will know through this that we are 'dwelling in Rén' as Confucius suggests. For example, if we often observe people giving up their seats on public transport to those who need them more, we are more likely to do the same because we are familiar with the action.

ACTIVITY

RECOGNISING AND CALLING OUT RÉN BEHAVIOUR

To dwell amid Rén in our own practice, as Confucius suggests, we should call out Rén behaviour when we see it. Try to recognise acts of kindness and compassion when you see them in others, or when friends invest time in self-cultivation while avoiding desires, or when we see others appreciating quiet moments in their lives.

As we follow our own practice, we can look out for others who might act positively, reflecting the area that our practice is focused on, and encourage, support or even just compliment them. Recognising Rén in others, and encouraging it where you can acts as a reminder for our own journey.

RÉN ONLINE

In the previous section on Emotional by nature (page 56), we considered how social media interactions mimic successful live social interactions and release hormones that make it pleasurable. This habit encourages interactions that are transient and difficult to develop more fully, though not impossible. The overabundance of transient interactions makes recognising Rén online a more difficult task.

From Driven by drama: harmful pleasures (page 87), we learn how drama hooks us into stories purely for their emotional experiences. Online, interactions picked up by the social media platforms' algorithms are the more popular ones, which tend to be driven by drama. When we see them, we are often compelled to engage, to add to our emotional 'high'.

To find Rén online, we need to re-humanise the representation of people in media and technology. Instead of following snippets of drama, we can find and nurture more meaningful connections. In the same way as we would in real life, we can be supportive and encouraging to others. The tweet below by the writer Aaron Corwin perfectly highlights the Twitter habit of 'doomscrolling' by reaching for the opposite, which he terms 'hopequesting':

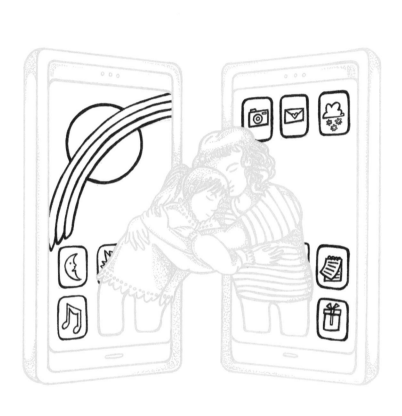

You're not doomscrolling, you're hopequesting.
You need those tiny pieces of joy from seeing friends and strangers share their art, their good news, their wacky unique selves.
We need light to live. And we find it in each other.

AARON CORWIN, TWITTER,

6 OCTOBER 2020

This is our modern-day search for Rén as we try to get back in touch with the basics of humanity, to successfully connect with others, through new technology. Finding Rén online will help us navigate away from the 'harmful pleasures' rife online and allows us to practise being Rén by putting technology in its rightful place, as a tool and not a way of life.

ACTIVITY
ONLINE MINDFULNESS

When you are online and you come across conversations that are trending, check if they provoke extreme responses, perhaps either fully in support of or against something. Recognise the drama in play and refrain from engaging.

When you find yourself conversing with someone online, try to engage with that person fully, as you would a friend in real life. Try spending more time building fewer relationships online than seeking 'likes' on your activities.

Practise to 'aspire and not desire' when online too. For example, seeking 'likes' is a desire that relies on the actions of others, whereas aspiring to create more meaningful and thoughtful content can reflect your Rén study.

BEING CONTENT WITH RÉN

> Is Rén truly unreachable? When I wish to
> be Rén, Rén will come to me.

THE ANALECTS 7:30

As we come to the end of this first part of the book focusing on Rén and ourselves, we should be reminded by Confucius that being Rén is a commitment to a lifelong practice. As Confucius said, when we wish to be Rén, Rén arrives. This highlights the ease with which we can begin our practice and the elusive nature of Rén, which requires dedication and effort. And when we are committed to Rén, we can find contentment in our practice.

To recap, we build Rén in ourselves by:

- Developing our self-awareness through mindfulness;
- Treating ourselves with kindness through acts of self-care that improve ourselves and our habits and lifestyle (self-cultivation);
- Learning how to manage ourselves through our individual preferences (rewards and emotional management) and understanding how we can apply change to our habits more easily;

- Understanding what it means to be human and what kind of impact modern life has on human traits;
- Opening up to the world around us, so that we may begin to recognise and embrace Rén.

When we feel that we are comfortable with our practice and are building Rén in ourselves, then we can proceed to include our family and friends, and the wider world. We need to do this remembering that Rén begins within us, and thus, our practice needs to be grounded within us. If we have any doubts or uncertainty at any point, returning to Part One helps us reorient our Rén journey.

There is nothing selfish about looking after yourself first. Only if you are happy will you be able to make those around you happy.

HAEMIN SUNIM
LOVE FOR IMPERFECT THINGS:
HOW TO ACCEPT YOURSELF IN A
WORLD STRIVING FOR PERFECTION

ACTIVITY
JOURNALING

Consider developing a habit of journaling to complement your practice. Journaling isn't only a mindfulness tool to help us get to know ourselves better. It can be a habit to organise our thoughts and daily lives – when used well, it can alert us when we have a change in our emotional and mental state.

Amalgamate previous activities into a variety of daily rituals that will further explore your self-awareness through mindfulness. Note down aspirations and build them into your personal development plans. Use the journal to reflect on your journey to being Rén.

To add variety to your mindfulness practice, try free writing to give yourself space and freedom for self-expression. This is also useful for when you are feeling particularly clouded with emotions, without clarity of thought. Sitting down to write with pen and paper (perhaps using your journal), set yourself a timer of 10–20 minutes. As soon as you begin writing, do not lift the pen, do not stop, even if you run out of things to say, keep writing words that pop into your head, even repeating them, until you find your next thought and continue. When you're done, put your journal away and only read it again after a few days.

If you keep clear journals through the years, you could also look back on past journals to remind you of the journeys you have taken to improve yourself. As part of your Rén practice, being able to reference and see clearly the positive changes in your life will encourage you to keep going.

PART TWO

RÉN

AND FAMILY AND FRIENDS

UNDERSTANDING POSITIONS AND RELATIONSHIPS

The learned do not overstep their bounds.

THE ANALECTS 14:26

NOW THAT WE ARE GETTING COMFORTABLE with our internal journey to becoming Rén, let us explore Rén in human nature and as part of our society. As humans, we have to navigate the world through our own nature and biological instincts, alongside the social constructs within our communities. Confucius teaches us how we can fulfil our role in this world by being Rén, responsibly and ethically, with kindness and compassion.

In Part One, we learnt the basic understanding that as social beings, our actions and choices have consequences for the people around us. When we are Rén – and our actions to our family and friends and the wider community are kind and considerate – the consequence is that this goodness will prevail and grow outwards, penetrating the wider societies around us. To simplify, Rén is contagious! And when our environments flourish with Rén, it provides opportunities for us to thrive, creating a positive cycle that returns individual benefits.

Confucius saw all social groups as interconnected and political. Whether a family, or a school, a workplace a government office, he believed that we all participate in politics – not in governance directly, but in activities that create positions of hierarchy. He was very aware of the structures in our society and our positions within it, and links this to our social function. This next stage in our understanding and practice of Rén is thinking about our place within the societies around us.

FAMILY ROLES AT THE CORE

> It is rare for someone who is filial to their
> parents and respectful of their elders to
> oppose their superiors. And it is unheard
> of for someone who dislikes opposing their
> superiors to start a rebellion.

THE ANALECTS 1:2

The family structure becomes the starting point in Confucius's teachings. In a family, the parents have responsibilities as guardians: to nurture, care for and teach their children. The children in turn have responsibilities as followers: to respect the parents, to learn and practice their teachings. And between siblings, there is responsibility to help and support each other, as collaborators do.

Once understood, the concept of the family structure can be applied to larger contexts, such as our community, our country and even the cosmos (universe). It has been documented that Confucius addressed the emperor as the 'son of heaven', establishing the great ruler's filial responsibilities as being to the 'Heavens'. He believed that the emperor is to be guided and nurtured by the 'Heavens' while learning from those 'Heavens'. And trickling down,

Confucius saw the emperor's role as the ruler-father and the magistrate (the government) as ruler-mother, each with their own set of responsibilities to the people (children).

Though in the past there were almost certainly clearer divisions of responsibility between a father and a mother, I find this division unhelpful in our world today and therefore I am applying a more modernised idea of the parent – whose responsibilities encompass the traditional duties of both parents and possibly more – to the interpretation of Confucius's teachings. This, I hope, will simplify the understanding of the roles as well as acknowledge the complexities of modern relationships and responsibilities. So, in Rén, we only need to understand three basic roles that stem from a nuclear family: parent (guardian), child (follower) and sibling (collaborator). Confucius taught that our function in society, no matter what the situation, will always be in the capacity of these three roles. And as in any family, if members perform well within their roles, the family then functions harmoniously as a unit.

NO BIG NO SMALL

'No big no small' is a Chinese idiom that I grew up hearing in all the dialects that my family spoke. My father said it in Hokkien, my mother in Hakka, together they said it to me in Mandarin and I watched our favourite Hong Kong soap stars say it in Cantonese. It is a commonly used phrase that no one in Asia can escape. In Malaysia, even if you don't speak any of the Chinese languages or dialects, you would have probably learnt the idiom in the English direct translation.

'No big no small' means having no recognition of seniority, or no understanding of your position or role. It is about understanding what your boundaries are depending on your role in a situation. It is usually used to criticise a lack of respect to elders. For example, I was told it when I talked back to my parents, or when I scolded my sister who is five years older than me, or if I interrupted an adult conversation. From a young age, I learnt my place in my family and in society.

As children growing up in East or South East Asian households, we understood that being told 'no big no small' meant that our behaviour had crossed the line of respect. Often, it would bring a sense of formality to the situation, which would keep our behaviour in check. Though the phrase might seem to act as a way to keep children quiet, as we grew up and understood more of the intricacies behind social behaviours, we learnt to readjust our actions so that we could communicate respectfully – properly.

ACTIVITY
FAMILY STRUCTURES

Consider your own nuclear family. What is the parent-child dynamic like (with you as the child, and/or you as the parent)? And if there are siblings, are there clear hierarchies between them? Now think about your closest relationships at work:

- Do you have a manager or supervisor or boss? How do you feel considering their role as a guardian to you?
- Do you manage a team or trainee or assistant? How do you feel considering their role as a follower to you?

If you are a part of other communities or social groups, try mapping the structure of the groups with the three roles: parent (guardian), child (follower) and sibling (collaborator). Can you place everyone with a role?

MULTIPLE ROLES

I have multiple identities. I'm British.
I'm Pakistani. I'm a Muslim. I'm a writer.
I'm a father. And each identity has rich
overtones. So I must be careful to look
at your identity, and that of others, in
the same way.

ZIAUDDIN SARDAR

In the example of the emperor in the beginning of this
section, Confucius highlights the fact that we always hold
multiple roles – as a follower, a guardian, a collaborator.
The emperor was a follower to the 'Heavens', while
being a guardian to the nation and a collaborator to the
magistrate. The emperor would also be a child to his
parents, and a parent to his children, and sibling to his
own siblings or cousins, or even good friends. Though he
held such a prestigious position, he still had to respect the
responsibilities of each role.

In all our lives, we begin first as a child. From there, we
grow into different roles while we learn the social protocols
that come with each of them. At nursery or school, we

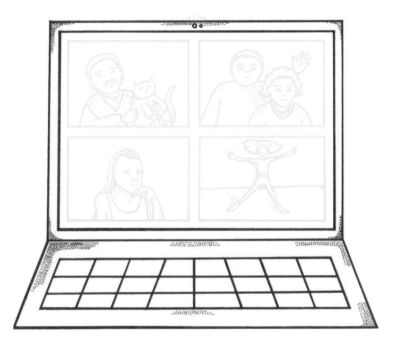

learn to respect our teachers, collaborate with friends and classmates, and we even learn to teach and look after those who are younger than us. At work, when we are first inexperienced, we learn from our managers or supervisors in our 'follower' roles. As we gain experience and confidence, we might become managers or supervisors ourselves, but often, we still have bosses more senior than us to guide us. And among our peers and colleagues, we grapple with sibling-like relationships that might complement or clash. However, the complexity of 'multiple roles' does not stop there. Within a relationship (between any two people) there may be multiple roles to comprehend. Let us take a parent-child relationship as an example. If the child grows up to become a medical doctor and the parent isn't one, in issues of health and medicine, the child will start to take on a 'guardian' role because of their advanced knowledge and experience. In the same way, if our best friend was an accountant (and we were not), it is likely that we would defer to their advice when it came to financial issues. These secondary roles are juggled depending on the situation and in accordance with the primary roles.

Though we often adjust how we treat others depending on the roles and relationships, we are not always conscious of our efforts or mindful about why we do. When we start to be mindful about how complicated relationships can be, we begin to appreciate the primary roles we have within specific relationships as the grounding roles. This can then guide how we act in situations that might introduce secondary roles temporarily.

In Rén, we use this understanding of roles and responsibilities to help manage our mental load and emotions. Knowing that we have fulfilled our duty allows us to feel content that we have honoured our role and thus been respectful of (and kind to) others.

ACTIVITY
MULTIPLE ROLES

List some of the relationships that you have where you feel your role is unclear, or where you might have multiple roles. These could be a family member who is also a client, or an older colleague who reports to you, or a teacher who is younger than you. Consider what your primary role is in the relationship and in what situations that might change. If, in the past a change of role was required, were you able to adapt easily?

If you are unsure about what these relationships and situations could be like, below are some possible scenarios:

○ Have you helped your parents or someone elderly with technological issues such as showing them how certain apps work on their smartphones, or setting up their modem or Wi-Fi connection? How did you feel in the situation? Did you feel like you had the 'parent/guardian' role? Did you still treat them similarly to how you have always done before or did you behave differently?

- Were there other times when you had to teach someone more senior than you? How did you do it? Could you treat them as you would children, or did you have to be more patient and respectful?

- Have you had someone younger than you teach or help you with something that you are unfamiliar with? Were you able to let them guide you as you would someone older? Were you able to respect their opinions and actions?

GRADATIONS OF LOVE

> Life and death are fated, wealth and status
> are decreed by the Heavens. The learned
> is always dedicated, vigilant, respectful and
> polite. In the world within the Four Seas,
> everyone is their sibling.

THE ANALECTS 12:5

Ultimately, Confucius taught that society should be treated as our extended family, but we should give close (actual) family members priority in treatment. It would be difficult to treat everyone who is a 'follower' to us in the same way as we would treat our own child, or everyone who is a 'guardian' to us in the same way as we would treat our own parents. In our lives, there are those for whom we would do more, such as cook and care for, even support financially, and those we would feel are not that 'close' to us. Confucius saw this as 'gradations of love', which depends on how we are positioned in a relationship.

If we imagine ripples of water, the clearest ripple in the centre would be our own family and as the ripples move outwards and fade, they reflect relationships in our lives that are less close, perhaps with extended family, friends and then colleagues and acquaintances. How we organise the people in our lives within these gradations is different, person to person. Some of us may have very close relationships with friends or colleagues. Then there are those of us who have estranged relationships within our own families. There are many circumstances that may cause us to consider the gradations in our communities in a certain way that might be different from others.

In the parent-guardian role, we might place our own parents in the closest position, moving outwards to our grandparents, in-laws, certain aunts and uncles, perhaps. Then, we might have our favourite teachers, managers and bosses. In the child-follower role, we would place our children (if we have any) first, then perhaps nieces or nephews, some of our students (if we taught), or junior colleagues whom we have trained. The most popular is likely to be the sibling-collaborator role, where most of our friends, colleagues and peers would be listed. For me, in my sibling-collaborator circle, I will list my sister and my husband in the innermost circle. Moving outwards, I have my best friends – some are also my closest colleagues – and my siblings-in-law. Further, I will have some of my cousins and friends. This will repeat until the outermost circles would just be acquaintances.

The gradations we place on our relationships will help us better understand the levels of responsibility, and decision-making. Like teams, we are accountable to our innermost circles and the levels of obligation decrease as we go further out.

ACTIVITY
ROLE AND RESPONSIBILITY

Try listing all the people who are in your innermost circles (your closest relationships) in their different roles. Being mindful of your role in the relationships (guardian, follower, or sibling), consider what you feel are your responsibilities or obligations towards them. How far would you go to help and support them?

RÉN AT HOME

On filial piety: Let your parents' only worry be of your health.

THE ANALECTS 2:6

S TARTING FROM OUR OWN SELF, Confucius placed the most emphasis in his teachings on self-cultivation. As we learnt in Part One, to become Rén, we need to concentrate on what we can control or change, and that is ourselves. Even within our nuclear family, we maintain this focus on ourselves by aspiring to fulfil our role(s) as best we can.

Because our priorities and aspirations will be different depending on the roles we have, it is very important to know what our roles are and to be aware of how we are fulfilling them. Confucius paid close attention to the values of respect and duty, which we will explore here.

'BE GOOD' OR 'GUĀI'

In my daughter's nursery, they have monthly 'value words' that they teach the children. Recently, I was excited to see that Rén was the word chosen for the month of October. Here, the translation they used to teach the value of Rén was 'be good'. The phrasing that is also a call to action that suggests 'I will be good' reflects the practice of self-cultivation. For children, the first step towards self-cultivation is to learn and being good reflects the ability to listen, understand and apply the teaching in practice. This is often interpreted as obedience or being well-behaved, or even clever or bright.

When we are a child or follower, to become Rén it is important that we learn to manage ourselves well so that we do not give our parents or guardians any cause for concern. As a child or follower, if we are well-behaved, it shows our dedication to learning from our parents or guardian. Our responsibility to them in this case is to be good children or followers.

As a parent to a young child, I'm constantly worried about her physical and mental wellbeing, but I understand that the more she is able to manage herself independently and properly, the less I worry. And so, in my role as a parent, I try to equip my daughter with knowledge and skills that will help her to achieve this. This can be through daily habits like teaching her to spot physical dangers, or more subtle skills like learning to make ethical and moral judgements. I also find myself reflecting on my experiences growing up, where I found my parents or teachers (those in guardian roles) too strict. I remember not being allowed to walk to the local shops without an adult present even though many of my friends did when we were just seven, or being pressured to achieve good results in school. Looking back, I can understand that all they wanted was for me to be able to show that I had learnt from them well and was able to manage myself responsibly, so that they wouldn't worry. Thus, when we are in the child-follower role, being respectful and understanding that our parent-guardian (at home, at work, or even elsewhere) has our best interests at heart helps us identify the motivations behind their instructions. And where this isn't clear, we can seek to clarify it with them.

ACTIVITY
ROLE SWAP

Parents or children who are up for some creative fun can try swapping roles for an hour or two one day. Playing the different roles helps them understand what the roles entail, even when it is just a game!

FILIAL PIETY

> The learned masters the foundations first –
> once established, the Dào is born. Filiality
> and respect for elders are perhaps the
> foundations of Rén behaviour.

THE ANALECTS 1:2

The teaching of filial piety is perhaps the most complicated yet persistent teaching of Confucius. People of East Asian heritage worldwide still practise and teach filial piety, generation to generation. This involves respecting or being filial to parents and elders. There are of course many interpretations of what it means to be filial now (after over two millennia), but generally, we recognise it as caring for and respecting our elders.

In Asia, it is commonplace to find many generations living under the same roof. When parents become old, it is the responsibility of the family's children to care for them. This is often practised in the same way as parents are expected to provide and care for their own children when they're young.

Confucius taught that to become Rén, we need to understand the depth of the parental connection and respect it. And through this respect, being filial is to care for our elders compassionately, which includes helping them to grow and learn through old age in a respectful manner.

RESPECT AND OBEY

In Rén, do not be afraid to surpass your teacher.

THE ANALECTS 15:36

A child shouldn't be rude to their parents out of respect for the fact that their parents gave life to the child and provided and cared for them until they were old enough to fend for themselves. If the parents were in any way wrong, first and foremost the child needs to take time to understand it. And once they have understood the situation as clearly as they can, they should try to encourage change through their own actions and to engage with the parents compassionately. In proceeding as kindly and compassionately as possible, we start to recognise and respect the depth of each relationship and so we are able to act accordingly. If the child is unable to understand or if the parents have behaved in an unacceptable manner, being respectful as we try to work through the differences will still help ease the situation.

The teaching of filial piety today is often misrepresented as blind obedience. In Rén, Confucius did not want us to blindly follow those in the parent-guardian role. Our practice begins from within ourselves and so we need to reflect on the lessons with which we are presented by our parent-guardian and take them into our own consideration and action. If there is conflict or disagreement, it is okay for us to acknowledge it and to accept that our practice in becoming Rén has surpassed that of our parent-guardian. Confucius separated the concepts of respect and obey, meaning it is possible for us to disagree and disobey while being respectful.

ACTIVITY
RESPECTFUL DISAGREEMENT

Have you previously had an open disagreement with your parents or someone who is a guardian to you? How did the situation play out? Do you feel like you gave them the respect they deserved in the situation?

Do you have something about which you disagree with your parents or someone who is a guardian to you that you have not told them about? Imagine a conversation with them about it: how could you disagree respectfully?

PARENTAL DUTY

> In leadership, if one sets an example by
> being honourable, who will dare not to be?

THE ANALECTS 12:17

When we are in the role of a parent or guardian, we need to remember that respect and obedience are two separate notions. If someone under our care does not obey us or has contradictory beliefs to us, it does not mean that they are wrong or that they are bad. Often, they might just have a different understanding or perspective. We need to keep in mind that our role as a guardian is to guide and nurture, and that we need to do so through our actions, for Confucius believed this inspires similar actions.

How we approach disagreements with those who are our guardians provides a model for the actions of those under our care on how they should approach disagreements with us. A guardian guides through their actions, a moral guardian paves the way for their followers to act morally. A filial parent who cares compassionately for their grandparents will pave the way for their children to be filial in imitation.

ACTIVITY
WORKING THROUGH DIFFICULTIES TOGETHER

If you find yourself in a position where you need to point out a fault or issue with someone who is in a guardian position to you (more senior than you), first try and engage fully. Listen without offering advice or comments and try to put yourself in their position. When you truly begin to understand their perspective, you may start to help them understand the impact of their fault or issue and in doing so, you can make their journey in dealing with it more comfortable by working through the changes they need to make together and at their pace.

When your child or someone in the position of a follower to you is being difficult – disagreeable, throwing a tantrum, or being emotional – be compassionate and try and empathise with why they may be doing so. Spending time engaging with them earnestly may reveal more of their nature and allow you to work through their difficulties and misunderstandings together.

RÉN AT WORK

Be a role model to those who follow you.
Disregard minor issues and promote those
who are outstanding. Those who you miss
will not be passed over by others.

THE ANALECTS 13:2

I N RÉN, WE LEARN THAT ALL SOCIAL GROUPS (from relationships and communities to organisations) are political. This isn't in reference to strategy or tactics, rather, it shows us that there are structures in place. These structures influence the development of our identities in the same way we influence others' identities, as we constantly navigate how we engage with people and the world around us.

It is unfortunate that modern-day politics has created a synonymity with the profession and corruption and greed, when the concept of governance should identify with nurture and care instead. In Rén, we need to remember that to Confucius, the role of those who govern isn't that different from the role of parents – the responsibility is to nurture those in our care through education and kindness. And through the role of the parent, we learned that upright leadership will encourage followers to be upright too.

In the past, when I worked at a small office of about 50 employees, I remember that most of us who were in junior positions would not leave before our managers at the end of each day. And when we did, we felt an obligation to justify it to our manager, letting them know the reason. It is easy to see this as a rigid organisational culture, but I believe that most of us, when in a new environment, would look to those who are more experienced for behavioural guidance. When we join an established social group, for example, we ask the older members about the group's structure and culture, or we might spend our first meetings watching and familiarising ourselves with how the group functions.

As humans, we enjoy a more fulfilling connection with those with whom we have behavioural synchronicity. This promotes social cohesion, which is important for community stability, which in turn is important to human structures. This is why for Confucius, the onus of behaviour within the community (family, organisation, nation) is on the leader(s). When a leader is able to lead with kindness and compassion, they will inspire their followers to do their best and want to improve themselves further. But if a leader creates conflict and pain in their way of management, those who follow will not be as averse to opposing or rebelling, thus generating more conflict and pain.

KIND AND COMPASSIONATE MANAGEMENT

> The learned helps others be their best, not their worst. The petty-minded does the opposite.
>
> THE ANALECTS 12:16

In one of my past jobs, I had a manager who often made cultural faux pas when talking to me about things relating to East Asian. I had never been annoyed or angry with her as she was always kind and compassionate to everyone around her; I was aware that her faux pas were accidental. Her intentions were pure. Her Rén personality made it easy for me to respect and be filial to her, in that I was able to talk to her amiably about her actions so that she could learn to correct her ways and avoid future mistakes.

If we are managing employees, Confucius reminds us to promote the human values that we want to encourage. In our modern work lives, we are often measured by 'targets' based on productivity or profits, which might overlook more important human values. Whether from Rén, or other ethics and practices in organisational behaviour that are important to us, we need to bring values that are important to us, such as honesty, kindness and diligence, to the forefront of how we manage.

Someone who is Rén also helps others to promote and perfect their good characteristics. If a leader spots someone who is a good team player, for example, they will help them build on and strengthen this in their work. If a leader spots a team member who achieves high sales or production values by appropriating others' work without credit, even though it benefits the team or organisation, the Rén leader will not encourage this behaviour. The parent-guardian role requires that we lead by example, drawing attention to the values that we would like our community to reflect.

ACTIVITY
MATCHING VALUES

In your work (whether it is for a corporation, an organisation, with collaborators or with clients as a freelancer) consider what values (morals and principles) are important to you:

- Are you also able to determine what values are important to those you work for/with?
- Do you think they match?
- How do you feel about your answer?

INSPIRE, DO NOT FRIGHTEN

The learned provides what is beneficial –
is that not being generous and not wasteful?
They delegate tasks that complement skills
– who will complain? If they desire Rén and
achieve it, how are they greedy? If they are
respectful and courteous to everyone, are
they not dignified but not arrogant?
When the learned holds themselves well
and looks on in reverence such that others
stare up at them in awe, are they not
inspiring but not fearsome?

THE ANALECTS 20:2

The ideal Rén manager or leader is someone who inspires and does not instil fear in their staff. In a work environment, we can often feel under competitive pressure to perform, to ensure that we do not lose our jobs, which would in turn affect our income and livelihood. Often, this pressure is out of our control and is affected by the stability of the various industries and their job markets. The role of the leader is not to add to this fear, but to nurture and educate so that their staff can flourish despite market pressures.

In the psychology of fear and anxiety, we learn that immediate fear forces a fight-or-flight reaction, but a potential fear creates anxiety that can be crippling to action. In most work environments, it is the latter that we experience and this constant anxiety for the safety of our jobs might cause us to panic every time we receive a message from our manager, or every time there is a formal announcement.

As a leader (in the guardian role), it is important that we are able to improve the working environment rather than cripple it. And by emanating kind and positive energy through our actions, we can create an inspirational environment that will not only improve our staff's experience and productivity, but our own too. This can be done through encouragement and reward, of course, but it will often be more difficult when it comes to considering how errors are corrected. Confucius teaches that a Rén leader who is 'respectful and courteous to everyone' in whatever situation they are in is someone who is dignified but not arrogant. Keeping good manners and consistent action (no matter who we are with) as a leader reflects a kindness, compassion and respect for those in our care.

In my first full-time job, during those initial few days in the office, I was told by numerous colleagues of how difficult my new manager was. I was the fourth person in the role in three years, they said. Needless to say, I started the role in fear. Because it was my first full-time job, I felt that I had to make it work, to prove to myself that I could do it, and this gave me the necessary courage and drive. Initially, I was jittery and afraid to take the initiative in case I got things wrong, but after my first month, I got to know my manager better and I became more comfortable as I learnt that, ultimately, her goal was for me to learn and be good at my job. She was strict because she put in a lot of effort to train me and she expected me to put in the same amount of effort to learn and improve. Looking back, she was concerned about properly fulfilling her parent-guardian role to me and she expected me in turn to fulfil my child-follower role too.

To this day, I am very grateful to this manager for she inspired in me the confidence to take on any work or project, showing me that all it takes is good grounding through research, critical thinking and hard work. Her work ethic still remains with me in every project I do. Though I didn't realise it then, her work ethic reflected Rén values, which built a strong professional foundation within me.

I later learnt that my manager had problems with previous staff members because of personal issues that created complications in the workplace. In my experience working with her, I believe that she had overcome those issues and managed to change her ways, which helped our relationship. In keeping to our roles of guardian and follower while we were working together, we developed a strong bond that helped me flourish, which in turn increased the company's output and improved the working environment in the office for other colleagues too.

This example also highlights the importance of keeping in mind our primary role in a relationship. Though we might find ourselves in situations where we are required to take on a different secondary role, using our primary role to guide us in our actions and behaviour helps to maintain a clear and strong relationship.

ACTIVITY
KIND MANAGEMENT

If you have people who work for you, whom you manage or supervise, try to reflect on the work environment that you have created for them. Is it a nurturing environment where they are able to learn and grow, or do you add to their fear and anxiety in any way? Do you feel that you are able to maintain your role as a guardian to your staff at work, at all times? And where you are socialising outside of work, do you still maintain the guardian role?

THOUGHTFUL STAFF

> When you meet someone better, try to become their equal; when you meet someone less, examine your own self.
>
> THE ANALECTS 4:17

Reflecting on the teachings from Part One (creating aspirations) and in the previous section on Rén at home (filial piety, *see also* pages 131–137), when we work for others who are our manager, Confucius teaches us to judge their actions so that we know whether to emulate or reflect them. In becoming Rén, we learn to judge others and not to criticise, but to be more thoughtful about our own actions. This is an important lesson in Rén as Confucius was actively against any call-out behaviour.

Previously, we learnt that to be filial towards those in guardian roles does not mean that we follow and obey them blindly. Confucius was clear that those of us who are practising to become Rén can and should judge others as it helps us be more thoughtful and critical about ourselves.

At work, if our manager or supervisor inspires us in their actions, we should analyse how we can emulate them and use their actions to inspire us to be better. However, if our manager acts badly, we should first survey ourselves to see if we reflect this bad behaviour too. Then, we should try to ensure that we never act in the same way. It is through thoughtful awareness that we can be certain that we won't be influenced or affected by negative and unworthy behaviour.

If we find that our manager's bad actions are hurting others, and we need to approach them about it or report their behaviour, then it is important that we do so in a proper manner. As they still hold the parent-guardian role to us, we need to respect them. We can do this by following proper channels as set out officially by the organisation we work for through organisation policies, or if that is lacking, we can seek employment advice from organisations like the Citizens Advice Bureau. This will allow them time and space to process the issue raised and to take the necessary actions.

ASPIRE (NOT DESIRE), CONTINUED

This reprises what we learnt in Part One to remind us to focus on setting goals that we can achieve with our own actions, rather than those that require others' actions. At work, for example, if we hope to achieve a promotion for a better role with better pay, we need to aspire to fulfil the requirements of the role rather than just setting the promotion as a goal. Desiring a promotion only places the focus on our manager or supervisor, who we want to give us the promotion, whether we are capable of fulfilling the requirements of the role or not. If we focus on aspiring and working towards acquiring whatever skills and experience the role needs, it gives us some concrete goals. When we take the initiative through our aspirations, we can also share this with our manager so that they may understand our goals.

Another way to think about this is to concern ourselves with the act of creation (within our control) rather than prediction (outside our control). At work, instead of speculating as to how our project or career will go, we should take action, concentrating on accomplishing each task well. And when we achieve recognition for our work (through a promotion or a pay rise), we will know that it is our due and we can be satisfied that it is because we are ready and able.

Where we might find managers and colleagues to be inspirational in their work, we can also aspire to follow in their footsteps to improve ourselves. When I left my first job, I made the decision due to many factors, but one of them was that I couldn't find anyone senior in the organisation who inspired me anymore. It was important for me to have a role model, someone I could learn from, and without that, I felt lost. This is what many might describe as being in a 'dead-end job', where I couldn't see where a long-term career would lead if I stayed on. Knowing that I needed a different environment to find new ways to learn and grow helped me make the decision to effect change in my life.

ACTIVITY
THOUGHTFUL CRITICISMS

Is there anyone at work that you feel is a bad influence? Consider their actions – what is it that they do that makes you uncomfortable, or makes you feel like they are problematic?

Look within yourself, have you acted similarly before? Would there be any situation in which you might act similarly? How can you avoid that and learn from this observation?

Is there anyone at work who inspires you? What are the qualities that particularly impress you? Do you aspire to develop the same qualities?

RÉN AND FRIENDS

Worry not about being unappreciated,
instead, worry about not appreciating others.

THE ANALECTS 1:16

ARLIER IN PART TWO, we looked at the specific elements of Rén that affect our relationships at home and at work. Now, we are going to explore what it means in friendships, through the siblings-collaborators' role. Although I have divided the different environments into their own parts (home, work and friends), it is important to remember that all relationships in Confucius's teachings can be considered as one of the three roles: parent-guardian, child-follower and sibling-collaborator. And depending on the gradation of love, we can manage the level of responsibility for the relationships accordingly, while being aware of any secondary roles that might be applicable in certain situations.

In Rén at Home and Rén at Work, we concentrated mainly on the parent-guardian and child-follower roles, which are important to both those environments. However, the sibling-collaborator role is almost certainly the most common of all the relationships we'll have throughout our lives. All the topics that we will discuss in this section about Rén and Friends can be applied to the home and work environments too as they are elements that will help with the sibling-collaborator relationships.

The sibling-collaborator relationship is probably the most complicated one to navigate. In these relationships we are constantly negotiating different roles depending on the circumstances, where someone might have the upper hand in certain situations, but not in others. With age groups being closer and hierarchies more fluid, sibling-collaborator relationships need to be grounded in love through mutual support and encouragement.

BEING WELCOMING

The learned does not discriminate nor create cliques, the petty-minded discriminates and creates cliques.

THE ANALECTS 2:14

clique /kliːk/
noun: clique; plural noun: cliques
a small close-knit group of people who do not readily allow
others to join them.

In the definition above, cliques are groups that forbid others to join in. This behaviour creates a closed-off environment with a secretive tone that is contradictory to the compassionate behaviour of Rén. Confucius promoted an openness and diversity in our communities with loyalty and trustworthiness as guidance.

The formation of cliques excludes and discriminates others, which then limits our opportunities to expand our community and knowledge. We become closed-off in our thinking, which contradicts the idea that in order to become Rén, we must practise self-cultivation through learning from others.

Cliques can also lead to bullying when people who do not fit into the group are 'othered'. The pack mentality gives members a false sense of confidence and power through strength in numbers. In Confucius's quote, he says that someone who is petty-minded or selfish creates cliques as a way to boost their self-esteem.

ACTIVITY
WHAT COMMUNITIES ARE
YOU IN?

Reflect on the different groups that you are in. How are they organised? Even those that are informal, are they open and welcoming to new members or do they have characteristics of a clique that go beyond the group's function*?

If you feel there are groups that discriminate or do not readily allow others to join in (despite showing an interest in the group's function*), consider how you feel about this. Perhaps try to work out why the group is set up as such and find ways to make it more welcoming.

* Many social groups are created around a function, such as reading groups or social sports groups, hobbies, etc. The group's function is the subject of shared interest for the group.

WELCOMING DIFFERENCES

> The learned does not accept a person for their endorsement, nor do they reject an opinion because of the person.

THE ANALECTS 15:23

Though the social networks we have today might seem a lot more complicated than in the past during Confucius's time, his observation of social function still applies. In developing friendships, we should not select friends because they like us, or because they often compliment us. We should not surround ourselves with only those who echo our opinion (which forms a clique) and reject the opinions of those we dislike.

Because our identities are moulded through our engagement with our communities and the wider world around us, our personal growth – through Rén – depends on our ability to learn from our communities, through compliments and criticisms alike. Our human nature sees us seeking validation through our social networks in all sorts of situations. We might seek compliments after a haircut, or support on an opinion that we voiced, or even getting 'likes' on a photo that we have posted. Though our friends performing these actions might make us feel good about ourselves, they limit our ability to grow. If we are surrounded only by those who echo our opinions (and disregard those who have differing views), then we will not get to expand outside of what we already know.

In order for us to grow our practice to becoming Rén and broaden our communities to expand our learning, we have to step outside our comfort zones and actively seek out new, diverse connections and communities. I have heard organisations complain that there is nothing they can do if the jobs they advertise do not attract many diverse applicants. The question would be: where are they advertising and to what audience? To use a different analogy, if we listen to pop music but would like to meet people who enjoy jazz, we should seek them out at jazz events or jazz communities, rather than our usual pop concerts and festivals.

Though it might feel odd to seek out new friends and connections from backgrounds that are different to our own, consider that not doing so means we are actively selecting only those who are similar to us.

ACTIVITY
DEALING WITH CRITICISM

Remember the last time you received criticism from a friend or sibling. How did you react and feel? Did you agree with the criticism and were you able to improve yourself through change, or did you disagree? If the latter, how did you react?

Now recall the last time you criticised a friend or sibling. Was the criticism necessary or welcomed? Were you kind and respectful in your delivery? How did you feel giving that criticism?

Do your friends find you approachable and easy to engage with? Do you think they are comfortable with you and happy to provide constructive criticism openly?

ACTIVITY
EXPANDING OUR CIRCLES

Try some of the following activities to expand your circle:

- When you find yourself with some spare time, sign up to participate in classes or groups to learn a new skill or hobby. If you are comfortable with new experiences on your own, do this alone. Otherwise, bring a friend along. In this new environment with new people, try and engage in conversational topics that you might not usually do, while maintaining an open mind to different ideas. If you're doing this online, make more effort to 'chat' or engage with new people in the class or group.

- If you enjoy specific genres of music, theatre or art, occasionally experience a different genre to the ones you already like. Before attending a performance or watching/listening to something online in this new genre, try and find out more about it first. You can read up about it online or at your local library, or if you know someone who already enjoys that genre, ask them to guide your initial experience and share their knowledge with you.

After the above experiences, take time to consider how you felt initially and how you felt afterwards.

RECOGNISING GOOD COMPANY

It is beneficial to make friends with
three types of people: those who are
straightforward, sincere and learned. It is
harmful to make friends with three other
types: those who are obsequious, insincere
and cunning in speech.

THE ANALECTS 16:4

Confucius was passionate about the role of friends in
his teachings and if I were to guess, I would say that it is
because in the three main groups in our lives – family,
work and friends – this is the one that we can actively
choose. To become Rén, Confucius was clear that we
must keep friends who will improve and support us in our
journey and practices. And we must in turn be supportive
and encouraging of them in their journeys too. The
great philosopher placed a lot of value on loyalty and
trustworthiness in friendship.

Confucius encourages judgement in friendship, as he
understood that our friends are the ones who will ultimately
help us with learning and becoming Rén. They are also

the ones who can disrupt our practice of Rén. Due to this, who we choose to be our friends, rather than keep as just associates, is important in our pursuit of becoming Rén.

In one of the academic research communities that I joined, I was quickly taken by how warm and welcoming the group was. Though I did feel out of place (being new to academia at the time), it was never a problem. I was encouraged to engage at my own pace when I wanted to and not pressured to do anything I wasn't comfortable with. When I contributed to the group, my contributions were always engaged with seriously and openly appreciated. I remember thinking that as an adult in my late thirties when I joined the group, it was the first time I had ever experienced such genuine openness and acceptance.

I met the founder of the group as a colleague and we have since become friends. And since my first experience with the group, I have been observing how the collective is managed and how much of it is influenced by my friend's behaviour. My curiosity stemmed from an aspiration to emulate my friend's Rén attitude. I wanted to be able to create safe and encouraging environments for my communities as he does, so people are comfortable to express themselves while learning and growing among peers and colleagues. In my observation, I found that through his consistent and wholesome attitude in the sibling-collaborator role, he has managed to influence those around him in the same way. The group itself has grown by numbers with more people helping out with the organisation, but I am pleased to say that it has not lost any of its original qualities.

I think it is common for us to question or be critical about the community or environment we are in if we feel uncomfortable or threatened, but when we feel comfortable or happy, we tend to just let things be and not look deeper into why this is so. In Rén, it is important in both instances for us to work on being more aware of the company we keep, first to learn and improve ourselves, but also to be able to recognise good company that will support our Rén journey.

ACTIVITY
WHO ARE YOUR FRIENDS?

In Rén, being critical of our friends is a reflective activity that helps us improve ourselves and not to criticise or judge others. Thinking of your close circle of friends, try and identify who they are and how well you know them, using the prompts below as a guide:

- Do your friends have qualities that you aspire to?
- Do you know what your friends' aspirations are? Are you able to encourage and support them to achieve their goals?
- Where you might differ in opinion with your friends, are you able to communicate and engage meaningfully about this difference and learn and grow from the experience?
- When you are in your various groups and communities, do you emulate a behaviour that you would like to experience from others?

BEING GOOD COMPANY,
OR JUST COMPANY

> Advise your friends loyally and guide them
> well. If they do not listen, stop. Do not set
> yourself up for rejection.

THE ANALECTS 12:23

In considering the social circles that we keep, Confucius suggests that we consider loyalty and trustworthiness as the requisites for friendship. These are the values that are expected among siblings and therefore among those who are in sibling-collaborator roles to us. This is both in terms of how we treat our friends and how we choose the close connections we have.

Being around people who are also on a journey of self-cultivation helps us in our own practice as we can openly correct our errors with no fear of judgement. And knowing that we will be able to support and inspire each other brings comfort that we are in a safe environment. In this unique sibling-collaborator relationship, Confucius asks that we are loyal to our friends and guide them well. As much as being with people who are practising to become Rén will help us improve, we need to also support others on their

Rén journeys and we can do so by lending a guiding hand where we can, through being supportive and dependable. When helping others to change and improve, we need to remember that for them to accept change within themselves, it often also means a need to change their communities too and this needs to be managed respectfully and sensitively. When successful, this will create a Rén environment which will encourage growth and improvement. However, Confucius also advises that we have a limit to the loyalty we extend, whereby if the other person isn't Rén and therefore does not recognise the support, perhaps even disrespecting our honest actions, then we should not persist. Being able to recognise when others are not Rén and are not open to learning, growing or changing through Rén is important in our practice too.

In Mandarin, there is a phrase that reflects how we can act when we are with those who are not Rén and are not open to improving themselves: 你说你的, 我做我的 nǐ shuō nǐ de, wǒ zuò wǒ de. Directly translated, it means: you say what you want and I'll do what I want. That might sound a little flippant and indifferent, but what is relatable and important to note is that our own actions are what is crucial. Going back to the lessons we learnt in Part One, we need to treat our interactions with others as a way to learn and improve ourselves and so if that interaction does not encourage or support our Rén journey (and the other person is not Rén), it is okay for us to let their words pass us by as long as we are true in our own Rén actions. Confucius does not ask us to ignore or remove such people from our lives, but he suggests that we do not invest our efforts further in them.

ACTIVITY
LOYAL AND TRUSTWORTHY

Consider how you are as a friend, using the following prompts:

- Do you think that you are loyal and trustworthy to your siblings and close friends?
- Can you recall any examples where you might have let your friends down?
- Can you think of ways in which you can improve and be a better friend?
- Are there people in your life to whom you are loyal and supportive, yet who use that support not to improve themselves, but for greed instead?

In friendship, who we keep close to us (and who keeps us close to them) is often a choice. How do you feel about the answers you provided above? Are there changes you would like to make to how you manage your friendships?

COMPASSION AND RÉN – LOVE WITHOUT EXPECTATIONS

> The Rén help others establish what they
> themselves wish to establish and help
> others achieve what they themselves wish to
> achieve. Thus, the best way to approach
> Rén, is through empathy.

THE ANALECTS 6:30

When we have a strong network of friends and communities, made of people who are sibling-collaborator to us, we can practise compassion in Rén through relationships by loving without expectations. Knowing that those closest to us are supportive of our efforts in self-cultivation, and like us, are loyal and place value in being honest, we can openly continue our study by focusing on our own actions. And without worry or hesitation, we can love those closest to us unconditionally.

When we are supportive of our communities, we can remove ideas of competition that fester in desire (to win or to be better than others) as we would support and encourage them to be successful and to flourish as energetically as we would do ourselves. As we practise to become Rén, as we grow to understand our own needs, we create opportunities for others to do the same so that our community may flourish together.

In the sibling-collaborator relationship, because it encompasses so many people in our lives – from our closest siblings and best friends to acquaintances, colleagues and new friends – we are perhaps more sensitive to the gradation of love in each relationship: to consider who are closest to us. Having a trusted network removes any unhelpful concerns around gossip or social-narratives in our communities that waste time and energy. It simplifies our main social interactions, knowing our immediate network is built around loyalty and honesty.

As we broaden our circles to welcome more people into our lives and create more opportunities for us to learn and grow, we practise Rén by offering loyalty and support. And where we find others who are Rén and are on a similar journey to us, we keep them close as inspiration and offer what we can to help them achieve their goals. We use our Rén actions to improve ourselves and to create a space where we can act upon the relationships we have, through Rén actions – to love the people in our lives without expecting anything back in return. In this way, we can give openly and freely.

To recap, we practise becoming Rén with our family and friends by:

- Being aware of our roles in relationships, whether as a parent-guardian, child-follower or a sibling-collaborator.

- Being aware of the gradations of love in different relationships – that though we have specific roles and responsibilities, the depth of our actions depends on the gradation of love (how close we are to the other person).

- Respecting and honouring those in parent-guardian positions to us and understanding that doing so doesn't mean to follow blindly.

  Inspiring those who are in child-follower positions to us, giving them space to learn and respond to our actions.

- Being welcoming to everyone and open to new experiences and connections that will help us learn, grow and improve.

- Recognising those who are practising to become Rén around us, so that we might encourage and support them in their journey and take inspiration from their practice.

RÉN

SOCIETY
AND THE
WIDER
WORLD

RÉN VALUES

The people can be made to follow a path,
but they cannot be made to understand it.

THE ANALECTS 8:10

PART THREE BRINGS A DIFFERENT perspective to Parts One and Two because we are no longer operating within the comforts and safety of the communities that we are familiar with or have chosen to occupy. Paying heed to the idea that we are social beings, Rén explores not only our direct relationships, but also the wider relationships we have with people in society, animals, plants and really all that encompasses the world.

The familial roles that we have learnt so far are still applicable, where depending on the situation and people's social positions, we still fall into one of the following roles: parent-guardian, child-follower or sibling-collaborator. However, the power dynamics in each situation are now determined by what is valued in the moment and this could concern status, seniority, wealth or even a combination of all three.

STATUS – Status is social or professional standing. Certain people such as celebrities, state officials or politicians have a public image, which accords them a different status to others because they are recognisable in public. Religious figures and uniformed workers, especially first responders such as the police, firemen and doctors, have this visual recognition too. Then there are others who might not be as easily recognisable but hold titles that have the same effect when made known to others, such as medical doctors, judges, Doctors, Sirs and Dames. In our society, status carries expectations about a person's behaviour, background, principles and philosophy.

SENIORITY – In many cultures and societies, reverence is bestowed on people who are older. The seniority that comes with significant life experience, especially when discernible – when someone looks older – is often assumed.

WEALTH (MONEY, KNOWLEDGE AND EXPERIENCE) – In our modern society today, wealth often goes hand in hand with a sense of privilege or power, sometimes even entitlement. Understanding where this wealth lies is important in certain circumstances, but the ensuing power should be perceived as a moral power and used only in that way (we will learn more about moral power later in Part Three).

In our day-to-day lives, we come into contact with various situations that juggle all three elements described above to determine our roles and how we should act accordingly. The status, seniority and wealth that we (or others) might have could hold us to be accountable for different forms of responsibilities. For example, when we are getting a haircut, the hairdresser is in a position of power due to their wealth of experience and skill in hairdressing. In this way, we respect their knowledge and treat them as the parent-guardian. Their role is to nurture by guiding us through a suitable haircut. However, in the same scenario, we might be considered to be in a position of power as the customer. Because we have the wealth (for payment), our role as parent-guardian here is just a small one, in providing the payment. Though small, it is our moral obligation to fulfil this social contract. In this example, we see the possibility of the many roles that we might hold at any one time and how we might constantly navigate between them. Note that breaking down this example – or any other situation in our lives – to just one power dynamic oversimplifies it as there will always be other factors in play.

To help us navigate these complexities, Confucius provides us with a set of values, which we will go through in this section. These will act as guidelines that we can follow. Confucius also notes that though it is possible to make people follow certain paths or take specific actions, the will to do so is not something that can be forced upon us. Instead, understanding needs to be driven from within ourselves, as we study and apply what we have learnt to our practice. It is when we understand why we should follow a certain path or method that we will be able to engage more deeply with Rén.

KNOWLEDGE

There are those who make do without knowledge. I am not one of them. To listen, understand and apply what is good; to observe and commit to memory – this is secondary learning.

THE ANALECTS 7:28

Learning is core to Rén and Confucius acknowledges that learning takes time and effort. During Confucius's time, they did not have the easily accessible collective knowledge that we have today. Education was only available for a select few who wanted to try for a role in governance.

In the quote above, Confucius suggests that he wasn't one of the sages who had innate wisdom but he had to work hard to learn. He did this through:

- Observation;
- Critical examination;
- Application through practice and memory;
- Sharing through teaching.

These processes are still applicable to us today, the only difference being that we have easy access to shared knowledge in the form of libraries, databases, courses and classes, all of which are available both online and in-person.

> To know what you know, and to know what
> you don't know – that's knowledge.

THE ANALECTS 2:17

In this provocative quote – because we can never know what we don't know – Confucius asks that we always assume a starting point of ignorance when it comes to knowledge. This allows us to constantly be in a position to learn and to grow.

Starting from a position of humility also helps us to avoid jumping to conclusions. Often, I have found myself wanting to react instinctively in discussions or situations, especially when they are designed to provoke. I learnt from behavioural science practitioners that people generally prefer information that validates their opinions over information that is accurate – it is human nature not to accept information (even if presented factually) that invalidates a pre-existing opinion. This means that growth requires us to unlearn ideas that we might previously have thought to be accurate. This is what drives us to react instinctively when provoked. To avoid this, I found it useful to create draft responses as taking the time to write forces me to engage with the topic mindfully. Often, having completed the draft, I would find where the gaps in my knowledge of the issue lie or that the reaction itself was unnecessary. I might even save the draft for a few days just so I can come back to it with a completely clear head. This habit works for me as I know I can be quick to react, especially when provoked.

Having a short temper means that my habit of jumping into arguments is a harder one to change. I have become more thoughtful in my response by managing to hold back and bite my tongue, but that action often gets interpreted as a quiet fuming instead. Though this is not great, for me, it is preferable to starting a full-on argument about a subject that I actually might not know enough about. When I was younger, I would want to have the argument just to have the final word, but I realise now that it is only my ego that drives this desire. In following Confucius's teachings, I have learnt to walk away from arguments, following it up with research to satisfy my need to learn. The goal is to build a breadth of knowledge, not to win arguments.

ACTIVITY
RESEARCH

Is there a global cause or issue that you have recently considered supporting? Make it into a research project for the next few weeks:

- Try and find out what the most reliable sources of information are on the cause or issue.
- Now analyse what you have found to determine what kind of engagement (support, action, advocacy) is most valuable to the cause or issue.
- If you are satisfied with the information you have found, engage through your own actions.
- Share through teaching and advocacy, if relevant.

ACTIVITY
TO ARGUE, OR NOT?

Think back to the times when you were in a heated discussion or argument. Did you participate passionately or did you hold back? If you participated, were you sure of your argument; did you have enough knowledge about the issue? How would you approach the scenario now?

When you spot a provocative discussion on social media, do you respond straight away with your comments? Have you ever drafted a response but not shared it? Consider whether taking time to learn more about the discussion would change the way you respond.

CULTURE – BROADENING LEARNING

> Why don't you study the Odes? They can
> inspire imagination, enhance observation,
> enrich communication and help express
> negative emotions. They can improve you to
> better serve your parents and your ruler. And
> they provide knowledge of flora and fauna too.

THE ANALECTS 17:9

In Part One, we looked at harmful pleasures that come from drama in our lives (*see also* pages 87–89). Here, I would like to explore what Confucius determined as beneficial pleasures. He said, 'There are beneficial and harmful pleasures. Music, rituals, praise of other's virtues and having worthy friends – these improve you.' This is in reference to culture and art, or *wén* 文, which can be translated as 'patterns of human civilisation'. The translation hints at the fact that wén – which I will refer to as culture and art – is able to reflect, communicate and engage with humanity itself and that the participation in arts (literature, theatre, music, fine art, sports) is an educational pursuit that allows us to understand humanity more deeply.

This interpretation of culture and art is not limited to Confucius's teachings and is widely accepted in the studies of humanities. Art and culture are often thought of as a society's repository of our collective memories. Our emotions are represented aesthetically through visual arts, music, theatre, literature, performing arts and more. And when we consume art and culture, it can evoke a response from us as it can communicate feelings from the specific period, place or event that it represents. This is also why art criticism is a popular way of using historic moments to explore how it might have been to live through those events. And this is how through art and culture, we are able to expand our learning beyond our own society or communities, geographically or historically. We can learn about things that are happening in other parts of the world or from the past.

Confucius said that a Rén lifestyle will include participation in the arts as a form of beneficial pleasure. This can be through learning, creating or even consuming art. It is pleasurable to consume art in the form we enjoy and it is beneficial because it can be a source of our learning, which deepens and broadens our knowledge. This knowledge becomes a part of our Rén practice of self-cultivation as it encourages connection with events, places, people and cultures that are different from our own experiences. As a form of entertainment, art and culture can trigger the release of endorphins (happiness or laughter) or dopamine (pleasure). Adding them to our lifestyle promotes a healthy practice.

ACTIVITY
DOING SOMETHING NEW

What kind of arts and culture activities do you participate in? When was the last time you learnt something new or experienced something different? Sign up for a workshop or class in something that you have never done before, perhaps at your local community centre or online (where there might be more free or affordable choices). Try doing this once every few months and if you're comfortable, do this on your own. Reflect on how you feel being in a new environment and learning a new skill.

If you and your friends tend to meet up often, suggest a different activity for all of you. Visit a museum or art gallery, or organise a creative writing afternoon or attend a sports event. Do something that the group does not usually do (or might even stay away from). Reflect on how you feel experiencing something new with your close friends. Does this expand the conversations of the group to include learning new things in future?

MORAL POWER

> There were four things the Master forbade:
> he refused to entertain speculation
> or demands of certainty, he refused
> stubbornness and acts of egoism.
>
> THE ANALECTS 9:4

In our day-to-day lives, we will often find ourselves in a position of power or superiority resulting from our status or role, or a position of wealth (through our skill, experience, knowledge or finances). When this happens, and we find that we are gravitating towards the parent-guardian role, we need to remind ourselves that this position of power is one of 'moral power'.

Confucius listed four things that he forbade with regard to moral power:

ONE MUST NOT ENTERTAIN SPECULATION: Learning and knowledge come first in Rén. No matter what the situation is, we need to approach it as if we do not have the knowledge and seek it before we act.

ONE MUST NOT DEMAND ABSOLUTE CERTAINTY: We need to treat the information and action of others as part of the knowledge that we accumulate in our learning and it is up to us to determine (by analysing the information) if we trust it. Because Rén insists we only look within and never desire anything from others, we cannot demand absolute certainty in situations or knowledge that is not within our control.

ONE MUST NOT BE STUBBORN: The inability to accept criticism, new information or a difference in opinion cripples our potential to learn, grow and improve.

ONE MUST NOT INSIST ON ONESELF: We need to place the needs of others before our own in any situation. And even in situations where we are in a position of power and in the parent-guardian role, we must not use this power to assert our thoughts or opinions over others.

These points are important to remind us how we should act when we are in a position of power. If we can heed Confucius's teaching, it ensures that we apply our strength in the situation as a parent-guardian to nurture and to guide. When in a position to help those who are outside our circle of family and friends, we need to remember to treat them with respect and engage fully to understand how we can help to improve their lives. Sometimes, this can just be a conversation, other times, it might be in referring them to organisations or charities that can help. However we take action, if we follow the Rén teachings, we can feel content knowing we fulfilled our role to our full ability.

A wonderful example of this is when celebrities use their platforms to promote activism. They are able to communicate the needs of the cause or movement they support to their fans and a wider audience, who might not have been aware of the issues in the first place. By using their celebrity status as moral power through their activism, they are taking the lead to contribute to the causes they are supporting. Some examples of this are: Angelina Jolie as the UN Refugee Agency's Special Envoy, Jameela Jamil's work in fighting for radical inclusivity and a culture without shame and Jane Fonda, a veteran activist who provides a platform for marginalised groups and educates the public on the issues of climate change, sexism and racism.

Though most of us might not have a similar status as that of a celebrity, we still hold positions of power and privilege in different ways – wealth of knowledge, experience, skill, status, age, etc. Being aware of these advantages can help us in our Rén journey to figure out how we can use them positively.

ACTIVITY
MORAL POWER

Take time to consider your roles in the wider world, outside of friends and family. Are you aware of any positions of power that you might have? How do you use your moral power in those situations?

Think about the different communities you belong to. Do you hold a position of power in any of them? Do you have a publicly recognisable status? Do you hold a title, are you a doctor or someone in a commonly respected position, or are you a celebrity? How do you use your position of power?

Can you think of anyone who is in a strong position of power, but does not use it as a moral power?

DO NOT DO UNTO OTHERS

That which you do not desire, do not do unto others.

THE ANALECTS 15:24.

This quote is known as Confucius's Golden Rule. He uses the negative – that which you *do not* desire, *do not* do unto others – to emphasise the need for compassion (to *not* hurt) and the necessity of moving away from desires. We must focus on our actions towards others, rather than what we want.

Ultimately, Confucius's Golden Rule dictates that we should not hurt others. If we do not like being slapped, we shouldn't slap others. If we do not like being insulted, we shouldn't insult others. The reason this teaching is called the Golden Rule is because it is taught in most (if not all) religions in our world. The phrase may be presented differently, but the principle remains the same.

The Golden Rule uses empathy as a guide as using empathy, we can relate immediately to a situation. If we hit someone out of anger, remembering the Golden Rule, we can empathise and relate to the experience of being the victim. This helps restrain us in a similar situation in the future and also guides us to a sincere response.

Empathy does not only help us recognise emotional pain, but also physical pain. When we spot a potentially harmful situation unfolding, we also react in empathy. Imagine a child playing on the street who is so engrossed in their game that they do not see a car heading their way. Naturally, we would want to run and steer that child to safety because the human body is built to process empathy – the ability to understand another's pain – in a similar way to the actual experience of physical pain. We suffer when we see others suffer. So, we run and help the child to prevent them from getting hurt (and to avoid suffering ourselves through empathy).

Rén dictates that we are good people, because naturally, we want to avoid pain, both in others and in ourselves. In that way, we do good because we want to feel good, but also because we do not want others to experience what we wouldn't desire for ourselves. This empathy joins together all of humanity and that humanity, as Confucius saw it, is at the centre of Rén.

ACTIVITY
MINDFUL EMPATHY

When you come across someone who has opposing views to you, try putting yourself in their position to understand how they have formed that perspective. If you would like to engage with them on the topic, first, consider how you might approach this. Then, consider if you would appreciate it if someone approached you in that manner. Remember, if you do not desire it, do not do it unto others – change your approach, if necessary.

If you find yourself getting angry at someone, first try to take control of your emotions and then consider how you should react by putting yourself in their position. Even if they are in the wrong, they might not be aware of it, or they might be reacting in the heat of the moment too. If you were them, would you like to be shouted at, or treated aggressively? Consider whether you would welcome your own actions before you act.

ON POLITICS

The learned hates those who points out others' faults, slander their superiors, and think themselves to be courageous but lack reasoning and understanding.

The Master hates those who pry and consider it wisdom, rebel thinking they're brave, and use insults as being direct.

THE ANALECTS 17:24

CONFUCIUS WAS OFTEN PULLED into matters of governance and politics. He abhorred behaviour that did not match that of Rén, which he considered to be irresponsible. In true governance, politicians (in the parent-guardian role) should be sensitive to the diverse population under their care and use their power to nurture and improve the lives of all those around them. As functioning members of our society, we (the people) need to also engage in politics to ensure that we appoint the right government to fulfil this responsibility and to encourage action on what we feel are the important issues in our community. However, politics in our world today seems to be about more than just governance as politicians use tactics and collaborations with non-political organisations to sway our views, often to gain popularity to get in power. And often, once they are in power, their actions might not always seem to reflect the needs of all the different communities they represent. This may deter people from engaging in politics today.

In the past, I have often avoided engaging in matters of politics as I find the conversations and platforms too aggressive. When I try to find out more, I often get overwhelmed and confused by the opinions of family and friends. More recently, using Confucius's teachings to guide my learning, focusing on facts and verified information has helped me engage more comfortably by avoiding opinions and misinformation.

With social media today, political rumours can be presented as fact and spread widely. Many people jump all too easily into accepting or believing those rumours, in what Confucius thought of as 'spying things out'. Doubtless, he would have been horrified by the use of social media to share unchecked rumours, but it is something that is concerning and widespread in our world today. It is important that we are diligent in our learning to ensure that we are able to pinpoint and unfollow any resources that may share unchecked rumours as truth or wisdom.

Often, reacting passionately to hearsay (whether in agreement or disagreement) may make us feel like we are taking action in a situation, but doing so without establishing an understanding of the situation or building up knowledge is purely an act of defiance. And Confucius hated the representation of defiance as valour. In politics, often we see rebellious action being cheered on in this manner. Returning to the concepts of respect and filiality, we learnt that Confucius did not equate them to obedience or compliancy. In the same way as filiality, Confucius expects us to give respect to the systems of governance and those who hold office. This respect does not require us to agree with them, but it does require that we take proper steps when engaging with them – especially against them. The participation in a cause needs to be understood for what the cause is trying to achieve and not just an urge or desire to rebel.

Confucius also hated those who used insults as an excuse for being direct. In communications, there is no practical use for insults other than to attempt to hurt the other person or party. In politics, it is an unprofessional action, which deflects the focus from important information and knowledge. The definition of the noun 'insult' is 'a disrespectful or scornfully abusive remark or act' and the key word here is 'abusive', which highlights there being a victim and a perpetrator. Commenting on opposing beliefs or disagreements need not be abusive for the point to be clearly communicated.

Both the actions of insulting and rebelling play on the part of human nature that seeks out drama for entertainment. Knowing this, various people, organisations or parties tend to use it to manipulate our views but having an awareness of this helps us to be more critical of our sources, so that we may be more clear-sighted in our engagement with politics. It can also keep our own actions in check so that we only add value to our community in our engagement with politics, rather than inflating the unnecessary drama.

ACTIVITY
EFFECTIVE POLITICKING

When engaging in research or conversations around politics, try to ignore unchecked outlets and sources that rely on drama to gain attention. Consider if this allows you to have a more objective perspective.

If you are drawn to promote your political stance publicly, ask yourself if you are being persuaded to do so by others, or if you are trying to educate others on a topic. Be thoughtful about how you present your stance. Remember, even disagreements or opposing views can be presented clearly and factually without creating drama.

RITES AND RITUALS

> Reverence without Lǐ brings burden,
> vigilance without Lǐ brings fear, courage
> without Lǐ causes chaos, candidness without
> Lǐ becomes insults. When the learned
> are dutiful, the community will flourish,
> when they do not forsake old friends, the
> community will be kind.

THE ANALECTS 8:2

During his time, Confucius was a master of *Lǐ* 禮, which can be loosely translated as rites and rituals. In Ancient China, people practised Daoist and Buddhist rites that act as a guide to cultural behaviour or social protocols. Confucius regarded these as important in our development towards becoming Rén. He saw the implementation of traditions and ceremonies as part of a practice that is structured by the communities that use it.

One example referred to frequently in *The Analects* is the ritual of mourning. In Ancient China, when a parent dies, their children are expected to go into a mourning period of three years, for a child takes three years before they leave their parent's arms. This reflection of birth and death, of respecting those who gave us life, in the process of mourning them, is a rite that teaches the understanding of our human nature (in grief), our social function (as a child) and of an action that is compassionate.

In every culture, religion, society or community worldwide, we can find such rites and traditions. They may differ in practice, but at the core, their function is the same. Rites are practised to help us maintain a sense of our humanity, a sense of Rén.

A common ritual in the world today is the celebration of birthdays. In most places across the globe, birthdays are celebrated with a cake and candles to represent the age of the celebrant. I am not one who enjoys such celebrations and as a result, I've tended to ignore my own birthday. During a recent birthday, however, my daughter pointed out that I did not get a cake or candles, which made her feel upset. Thinking about this, when we celebrated her birthday, I began to understand how important this ritual is. As children, we look forward to our birthdays to celebrate what we'll be able to do (as we grow physically and mentally), knowing the next year will bring new discoveries and skills. In my mean-spiritedness, I had forgotten what it is to acknowledge past experiences and to look forward to the new things that we will achieve in our lives. This is marked through the ritual of singing a 'Happy Birthday' song, blowing out candles and eating cake – an important celebration in all our lives.

A friend's son recently celebrated his Bar Mitzvah. My friend wrote a reflection after the event, which I was grateful to read, as it highlighted the importance of the ritual to him. Practised since the Middle Ages, the Bar Mitzvah marks the child's arrival at an age where he bears his own responsibility for Jewish ritual law, tradition and ethics. My friend described how the celebration reminded him of a wisdom that children have, from which adults often get distracted. And we should learn from our children's wisdom to keep alive within us the children we once were. In his reflection, my friend ended with a note that the synagogue has given his son and family a community, a sense of belonging, friendship and love. This echo of Confucius's teachings of Rén highlights the beauty in the practice of rites and rituals in our lives.

Rites and rituals also create a structure in which we can exert our values, while protecting us against undue actions that might hurt us. All religions and cultures have their own rites and rituals for this purpose and give us guidance on how to experience certain events. For example, when a baby is born, in Chinese tradition, we celebrate their 100th-day anniversary. This is a guide to the amount of time both mother and baby might need to recover from the birth, marking the 100th day as a good time to introduce the child to friends and family.

The vast amount of rites and rituals in our modern world can range from ceremonies (weddings, graduations, etc.) to holidays and religious events (Christmas, Ramadan, Lunar New Year, etc.) to movements such as Earth Hour, World Book Day and more. The use of rites and rituals penetrates all layers of our lives and society. As humanity grows and changes, we will develop more and more rites and rituals to guide us through different experiences in our lives. We will also forget old rites and rituals that may no longer be relevant. Through better understanding of the rites and rituals we observe, we can improve our lives by adopting ones that will help us become Rén.

ACTIVITY
LIST YOUR RITES AND RITUALS

Looking at your calendar, list the rites and rituals that you observe annually. Write down some information on the events to understand why they are important to you. Are there any rites and rituals that you do not currently observe but would like to? Find out more about them and add to your calendar.

DAY-TO-DAY RITUALS

Another form of rituals can be found in our day-to-day lives. Many of us have rituals at different points of the day to set us up for certain things. For example, after taking my daughter to nursery in the morning, I have a quiet coffee, which gets me in the right mindset for my day's work. Some dog owners might use dog walking as a ritual to contemplate or meditate if they have a lot on their minds.

In my work with writers, I have learnt that we are a community with a lot of rituals to help with our writing and productivity. Often, when we start a new project, many of us have a ritual of getting new stationery to mark the occasion – starting a new notebook brings a sense of beginning and the excitement of things to come.

Positive rituals can be a part of our mindfulness practice in becoming Rén. Understanding why we might want specific rituals in our life and mindfully making them a part of our daily routine creates a sense of purpose that brings positive energy. Daily rituals are a form of preparation for the task(s) ahead and understanding this means that we can employ rituals to more effectively develop our Rén practices.

Some examples of daily rituals include:

- Meditation, yoga, mindfulness activities
- Walking the dog or playing with pets

- Organising the home
- Sporting activities such as running, swimming and working out in the gym
- Journaling, blogging, free writing
- Mealtime rituals, including cooking and eating

ACTIVITY
MINDFUL RITUALS

Do you have a daily ritual that is a part of your mindfulness practice? If you would like to start a new daily ritual, experiment with prepping first. If it is journaling, for example, get a new notebook and pen and try to set a time every day when you can make a conscious effort to sit down and write a few lines either in preparation for the day to come or as a reflection of the day that has passed. To start a meditation ritual, find a good spot and make it comfortable and tidy. Depending on the type of meditation practice, you might like to light a tealight or burn incense, or have soft music playing in the background. For a running ritual, find a playlist and route that gets you excited to go out and run. Aim to create an environment that encourages you to enjoy the ritual.

RÉN PRACTICE

The learned is ashamed when their words overshadow their actions.

THE ANALECTS 14:27

As we establish our Rén practice, we can look to the values that we have learnt in Part Three as a guide to our conduct. Confucius believed that to become Rén, we do not depend on our status or wealth and it does not matter who we are or where we are from. Rather, becoming Rén completely depends on our conduct, our actions. And if we are ever unsure in our practice, returning to these values helps support our Rén journey. To summarise:

KNOWLEDGE – Learning is at the core of Rén as Confucius valued wisdom in our conduct. Our actions should always be based on reliable knowledge and where there is none or not enough, our first act should be to learn and gain knowledge.

CULTURE – Confucius encouraged participation in culture and art activities to broaden our learning with experiences outside of our own. A Rén practice values diversity as a source of knowledge.

MORAL POWER – Understanding that we all have moral power in different ways encourages us to be more righteous in our Rén practice. Power isn't limited only to those who are privileged and when used morally, it can transform our communities positively, which in turn creates opportunities for us to thrive in our communities.

DO NOT DO UNTO OTHERS – Reciprocity can inform our actions towards others. Confucius encouraged reflection on not treating others as we ourselves do not wish to be treated. The focus here is on our actions.

ON POLITICS – In matters of governance, politics should be without drama. Knowing that the drama we experience in politics is often a misdirection or deflection from the core issues allows us to engage more effectively with matters of governance in our communities.

RITES AND RITUALS – Confucius encouraged the practice of rites and rituals that help us navigate our social responsibilities better. Understanding the rites and rituals we have today helps us improve our Rén practice and creates an enjoyable daily routine for ourselves.

RÉN
TODAY

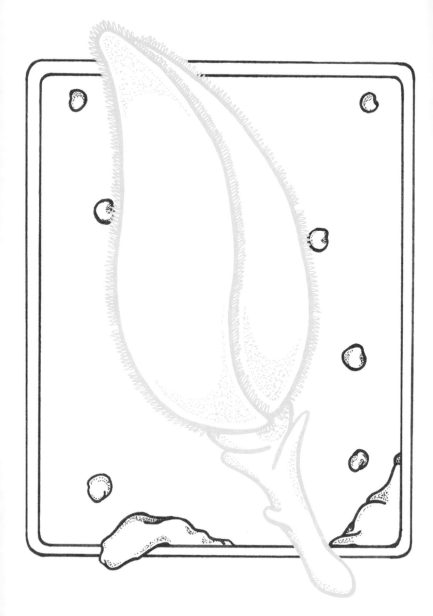

RÉN IN THE
TWENTY-FIRST
CENTURY

N THIS, THE FINAL PART OF THE BOOK, we will look at how Rén can help us make sense of the complexities of our society today, which is driven by the use of technology that permeates every aspect of our lives. Though Rén originated in Ancient China, in our wider world the values that Confucius placed on humanity still apply today and we can take comfort in our Rén practice to sustain a more contented and fulfilling modern lifestyle.

Due to the modern overload of stimulation – from news, entertainment, opinions, knowledge and ideas streamed into our lives through technology – we might often feel helpless and anxious, uncertain what we should or can do, perhaps even feeling guilty for not doing enough. Applying Confucius's teachings to our daily lives guides our thoughts and actions, which can bring reassurance that we are taking appropriate action – engaging with the world around us in a positive manner to the best of our abilities. Knowing that we are doing our best daily can alleviate anxieties and bring comfort and contentment to our mental and emotional health.

The following topics are collated to consider the modernisation of Rén and how Confucius's teachings and values are applicable and adaptable for the twenty-first century.

RECOGNISING COMPLEXITIES AND MULTIPLICITIES

Those who study with us might not share
our pursuit of Dào. Those who pursue Dào
with us might not take a stand with us.
Those who take a stand with us might not
share our ethics.

THE ANALECTS 9:30

N OUR WORLD, which now feels more globally connected
than ever due to information technology and high-
tech transportation, the differences between people
(opinions, experiences, background, etc.) highlighted

in our relationships (family, friends, colleagues and acquaintances), roles (parent-guardian, child-follower and sibling-collaborator) and alignment with others (gradations of love) come with a need to recognise the complexities and multiplicities among us. If we allow ourselves to be guided by Rén and by our human nature, we can find peace in how we approach the diversity in humanity – with open arms.

In Confucius's quote above, he highlights how long and complicated it can be for a relationship to truly develop between two people. It also highlights the fact that we can never truly know or agree with everything about another person.

If we work at a medium-sized or large company, we likely have colleagues who we know only through their job role and how they behave at work. Learning about their personal life or meeting them outside of the office might feel surprising, especially if it differs from the image that we had in our minds of them. When we are approached by a homeless person or a beggar, the experience can be somewhat similar in that we might treat (and judge) them as just a homeless person or a beggar without considering who they might be outside of that status.

This narrow perspective that we might have of people is limiting. In our interactions with those outside of our core community of family and friends, it is really difficult, or even impossible to get to know more about a person, as most of the interactions are limited to a specific situation within a short space of time. Confucius teaches us to be mindful of the fact that people are complicated and different. Even if we are unable to learn more about someone, keeping this in mind is enough to create a more holistic human representation of them – reminding ourselves that they are not just a homeless person, or just another office worker, for example.

Using this knowledge, Confucius encourages us to be Rén in our actions and treat others as we would a sibling – kindly and respectfully. Whether a situation requires us to engage with them or take any action to assist them or comply, we need to accord them kindness and respect. In the example of the colleague, we would not be rude to them or refuse engagement or friendship with them. And in the example of the homeless person or beggar, we would be kind and respectful in our interaction with them.

Rén practice does not assume that there are set responses to situations – in fact, the opposite is true – it assumes every situation is different depending on circumstances and the roles we are in. In this way, we are not expected to agree with someone because they are a colleague or to talk to and help every homeless person we come in contact with. However, to become Rén, Confucius demands that we try to be consistent in the way we interact with others regardless of who they are.

ACTIVITY
BUILDING A STORY

Is there someone in your life that you meet often, but you're only aware of what they do for a job – for example, your postman, or a colleague at work from a different team, or the barista in your local café? In casual interactions with them, try to learn more about them to build a fuller picture of their lives. I find that people open up a bit more when we share about ourselves in conversation first. For example, you might try saying, 'I'm currently reading this book [title]. Do you like reading?' Take time to learn about them and check-in on how you feel when you interact with them as you get to know them better.

ACTIVITY
MAKING UP A STORY

When you find yourself enjoying a quiet moment in public, maybe during your daily commute or while taking a stroll at a park, watch the people around you and make up stories about them. Have fun with the process and imagine how they might go about their day-to-day lives.

MODERN ISSUES

Look into those who are hated by the masses,
and those who are loved by the masses.

THE ANALECTS 15:28

WHEN WE KEEP WITHIN COMMUNITIES that are similar to us and we do not push ourselves to expand our knowledge, we end up creating an echo chamber around us that reflects what we already think (and do). It is difficult for us to be aware of this chamber as it creates a comfortable environment that avoids differences, diversity and disagreements – it is easy to get used to being in an echo chamber.

Social media and digital platforms are set up to create personalised echo chambers. The algorithms generate content based on databases of users' habits. Much like book and movie recommendations where we often get told that others who like this also like *These Other Titles*. Depending on the platform, some will throw in wild cards to try and entice you to generate more data for them to work with. Most of the time though, you are seeing what you're likely to want to see already.

Cancel culture, which is prevalent across technology platforms, can contribute to our personal echo chambers too. When someone does something that we disagree with, we might feel entitled to ignore or write off everything else they do. We might mute them online or remove them from our lives. Though this can very occasionally be advisable when dealing with bullies or trolls, if we find that we're doing this often, and to people who are sincere in their opinions, which might differ from ours, we should consider that we might be enforcing our own personal echo chamber.

The echo chamber creates a partisan perspective that goes against Rén, which encourages an inclusive and diverse environment. We need to actively pursue information outside of our echo chamber and hopefully in doing so, we feed our social media and digital platforms new data to tell the algorithms that we enjoy more diverse information.

ACTIVITY

EXPANDING YOUR KNOWLEDGE

How are you expanding your knowledge from what you are already interested in? Using trustworthy resources (for example, reputable news sources or academic institutions), try seeking out new publications or recordings of lectures and talks, sampling a range of topics.

On your social media platforms, follow a diverse range of accounts, refreshing the list often.

USING KNOWLEDGE – FINDING VICTIMS AND FOLLOWING PROFITS

To not know fate, one cannot be learned.
To not know Lǐ, one cannot act. To not know
language, one cannot understand people.

THE ANALECTS 20:3

I N LEARNING ABOUT ISSUES IN our wider world, we should assess what we learn, paying close attention to who is victimised and who profits (or is rewarded). This method of researching helps us assess the seriousness of the situation more effectively. When we learn about an issue, often, it might look like a straightforward argument that has clear right and wrong stances. Though we know that issues are generally more complicated and don't usually have clear black and white answers, often we fall for this binary thinking for ease of understanding. To overcome the need to become fully-fledged experts in every issue that we engage with, we can assess the issue by asking who the victims are and also who gains. Understanding issues in human terms also helps steer our actions with Rén.

An interesting example of this is the modern-day recycling movement. In the last few years, we have seen news about how our waste from the UK has been exported to China, where it isn't actually being recycled and is becoming a hazard to the locals. In this example, there could be two sets of victims: those who have to deal with our waste in Asia and UK residents who believe that we have been responsible with our waste and that our recyclable refuse was actually being processed. As to who profits, there are the parties that signed the waste export-import deal – those making money from the arrangement – and manufacturers of the products that generates the waste, who continue to make a profit, but seem to have little to no engagement with the waste processing. Understanding the issue in this way helps us make an informed judgement as to how to take action on the recycling movement. While we continue to learn more about where actual recycling is taking place, we can apply change to our own habits to help the cause – for example, start by reducing single-use plastics in our households. We might also push for a higher levy to be placed on single-use plastic products to discourage purchase, while encouraging manufacturers to consider other sustainable materials to be used instead.

As we continue learning about an issue, we might think of other victims and profiteers (for example, you might even be coming to a different set of ideas and conclusions to the example above) and we might also change our minds about what actions are best. Confucius considered this to be part of the cycle of growth – learning, understanding, applying, changing. Being critical about the issues in our wider world is key to being Rén as this knowledge encourages us to improve the world around us.

> There is no discrimination in teaching.

THE ANALECTS 15:39

While we engage with what is happening around us, it is important to note that in Rén, all humans function in the same way in our world, with no divisions. This means that when we are unable to relate to a cause or movement, we need to ask ourselves why it doesn't affect us. It might be because of privilege in our status, our ethnicity or identity, or we might just be unaware. When this happens, we may find that even though we feel unaffected, we are not a neutral party to the issue and that further learning is required. Going back to considering who might be the victim(s) and profiteer(s) as we learn helps us recognise our position in the cause or movement.

In Rén, because we are implicitly affected by our environment and community, we have to use our knowledge and our love of learning to channel energy into improving our world. This, in turn, will improve our lives.

ACTIVITY
BEFORE WE PARTICIPATE...

When you come across a cause or movement that has caught your attention, do your research first to develop a wider understanding. In your research, try to find the victim(s) and follow a possible profit route. Look into how you feel about the information and consider whether it moves you sufficiently to engage in it. If you know of people in your community who advocate the cause, try and find out why they're doing so to help build more knowledge in your research.

As you develop more knowledge about the cause or movement, do not be concerned about changing your mind on the victim(s) and profiteer(s), and how you want to engage, but be aware and take note of the changes. These should reflect improvement.

ACTION BEFORE WORDS: TRUTH, ALWAYS

The learned is cautious with their words.
Does that mean one who is cautious with their words can be regarded as Rén?
How can one not be cautious with their words when it is so difficult to turn their words into deeds?

THE ANALECTS 12:3

THERE IS A LOT OF FEAR and sensitivity in our public interactions today and this is only exacerbated online. With the openness of online platforms, it is easy to find those who agree with us, as well as those who disagree. And with online behaviour, it is commonplace to find trolls who react with insults, even threats.

With so many important causes and movements in recent years such as Black Lives Matter (a human rights movement), the climate movement (activism related to issues of climate change) and LGBTQ+ (a social equality movement) to name just a few, even when we do not speak up, we can sometimes feel pressured to do so. I have heard when activists have proclaimed that silence is consensus, silence is betrayal, silence means you are a part of the problem because silence means you are complicit. This makes silence highly problematic.

I am introverted and I do not like confrontations (online or in person), so keeping silent is my preferred stance. But that does not mean that I am keeping still. In practising to become Rén, I was glad to learn that Confucius teaches for us to be sparing of speech, to be cautious with our words. Confucius preferred action over talk, as action has a more direct impact.

Being self-aware, cautious and conscious of our speech goes hand-in-hand with Rén, which requires us to be honest and loyal in our actions. And like our actions, if we join in speech, we need to ensure that what we say comes from sound knowledge and is the truth, and how we say things (in our interactions) is always respectful and true – without embellishments that might distract from the message. This also means that just talking about an issue, especially online on social media, doesn't mean we are taking action. It can be a good starting point for awareness and research – to understand the issue better – but it should not be confused with actual engagement. Recently, there are many companies that have come under fire for jumping on the 'Pride bandwagon' during Pride month – a month dedicated to celebrating LGBTQ+ communities around the world. These are companies who launched Pride-month specific marketing and used the rainbow banner through the month, but do not have LGBTQ+ inclusive policies and practices in place. In the same way, many individuals might talk about these movements or causes, but they could be unaware of their own actions that might not be in support of them, even contradictory to them.

If you were to lead a grand army, whom would you like to take along with you? Those who fight tigers with their bare hands, wade across rivers, and are willing to die without regret – I would not want their company. Instead, I would want those who are thoughtful, approach affairs with caution and are capable of executing their strategy successfully.

THE ANALECTS 7:11

In thinking about our own actions, Confucius considers someone who is able to approach an issue thoughtfully and strategically to be Rén. In reckless behaviour, when consequences are not considered, it might cause harm and pain to others and in the long term. Confucius doesn't discourage activism, but admonishes against violent or risky behaviours. He believes that activism, like all actions, is best managed strategically.

Keeping in mind our own strengths, experience and knowledge, we need to first consider what possible actions we might be able to take for the cause or movement. How can we engage and contribute positively and effectively? As part of our practice, if we put in the effort to gather knowledge and learn about the causes and movements that are important to us, we can be reassured that when we are ready to take action, we are able to do so effectively based on our abilities and the cause's needs. We can also be confident that our positive actions will inspire others to follow.

ACTIVITY
EDITING FOR ACCURACY

Do you enjoy sharing online about causes and movements that you support? When you engage with online content, do you check the sources before liking, sharing or quoting from them? Consider editing what you share for more accuracy – limit yourself to only sources that are reliable, whether organisations or individuals. Often, we might find ourselves wanting to share a stranger's post even though we are unsure of who they are and their role in the cause. When this happens, refrain from sharing immediately and instead check for accuracy.

ACTIVITY

STRENGTHS, EXPERIENCE, KNOWLEDGE AND NEEDS

Is there a cause or movement that you are passionate about and would love to engage positively to support it? Here are some first steps to take:

- Take time to learn about your chosen cause or movement and develop a deeper understanding of it.
- Write down a list of your strengths, experience and knowledge that you think would be useful to the cause or movement.
- Compile a list of what you think the cause or movement needs.
- From those lists, consider what actions within your means would be most effective.

MANAGING
CHANGE

That I fail to be ethical, to learn, improve, and change – these are my worries.

THE ANALECTS 7:3

WHEN WORKING TOWARDS OUR **Rén** aspirations, we will need to change our actions, habits, beliefs and more as we improve and grow. This is part of the Rén journey that brings us fulfilment through our contributions to the world around us. Change is not only inevitable, it is also a force that can push us to be better, to become Rén. That is why Confucius focused so much on personal change.

In Rén, though we are integrated with the world around us, the change we want to effect is only within us: through our own actions. Even when we want change to happen around us, we only ever engage through change within ourselves. Using Rén values as guidance, our practice requires us to acknowledge past mistakes and to correct them and change our ways. Though this might not always be easy, doing so releases a burden within us knowing that we have fulfilled our responsibility, and helps us move on.

ACTIVITY
TRACKING CHANGES

Leave a notebook and pen by the side of your bed. Before you go to sleep at night, while lying in bed, run through your actions of the day and think about all your accomplishments in reference to your roles in each instance. If you notice a discrepancy in your actions, write down any steps that you can take to correct it; otherwise, acknowledge it so that you do not repeat it again.

Acknowledge the day you've had before going to sleep so that you may start the next day afresh.

ACTIVITY
CHANGE FOR A CAUSE

If there is a cause or movement that you are supporting or would like to support, explore how you can make a change in your actions, habits, beliefs, etc. for the cause or movement using the following prompts:

- ● Is there anything that I currently do that is in contradiction or harmful to the cause? How can I change this?
- ● Is there anything that I currently do that already supports the cause? How can I do more?

RÉN AS A
FOUNDATION

JUST AS CONFUCIUS WOULD NOT have been able to imagine the world in which we live today, let alone have any inkling that his teachings would survive and still be applied in the twenty-first century, we can expect our world to continue to bring us new challenges. I hope that Part Four offered reassurance that with Rén as a foundation to our way of life, we will be able to navigate any developments and obstacles that our future holds.

Rén reflects the framework of humanity, which thrives in positive and prosperous environments. And it is only natural for people to gravitate towards communities and places that seem to offer more or better opportunities. As we practise to become Rén, we inevitably create an environment that brings the opportunities we seek. In the same way, if we practise chaos, we disrupt our environment, jeopardising our own journey. Though the issues in our wider world might seem so much bigger than our individual lives, if we follow the Rén teachings, we can be confident that we will contribute positively.

CONCLUSION

There are three principles in the way of
the learned that I have been unable to
accomplish: in Rén, they are not anxious,
being wise, they are not confused, and being
courageous, they are not fearful.

THE ANALECTS 14:28

CONFUCIUS THOUGHT THAT THE perfect person is
someone who is Rén. Though he held humanity's
potential to such a high standard, he made it clear
in his teachings that Rén isn't something that any one
person can achieve. Rather, it is a journey of self-discovery
and improvements that one can commit to. He would never
admit to being Rén because he was constantly learning and
in that way, he set himself as an example to his students and
disciples – and now, us.

For me, Rén deserves to be practiced today because it is practical and it functions in a realistic and meaningful level. It never tries to engage with concepts of altruism because that is unrealistic – unnatural to human behaviour. Confucius regarded Rén behaviour as advantageous to the individual and encouraged his students to think that way. Understanding the benefits of our practice allows us to be more committed to it. Here, let's remind ourselves of the key lessons learnt in each part of this book:

RÉN AND YOU

Here, we learnt that Rén begins from within ourselves in the form of self-awareness and that acts of self-improvement and cultivation are a part of self-care – where we treat ourselves with kindness. We then explored what it means to be human and how we can achieve a state from which we begin to find fulfilment through our experiences of and our relationship with the world around us. We do this by appreciating harmony and peace and understanding that happiness and fulfilment are not rewards to be earned (or desired), but states of being that can be achieved through Rén. And when we open up to the world around us, we may begin to recognise and embrace Rén.

RÉN AND FAMILY AND FRIENDS

Confucius saw hierarchies all around us and he taught that using the core family structure, we can understand about the roles we hold and how we can fulfil them. The three roles in Rén are: parent-guardian, child-follower and sibling-collaborator. At home, we learn about filiality and respect. At work, we learn about nurturing, inspiring and acting with compassion. And with friends, we learn about recognising, appreciating and keeping good company.

RÉN, SOCIETY AND THE WIDER WORLD/REN TODAY

Here, we learnt that to become Rén does not depend on our status or wealth, and it does not matter who we are or where we are from – rather, it depends completely on our conduct, our actions towards others and the wider world. For this, we reviewed Rén values that can guide our actions. And finally, we explored how Rén can be applied to political and social issues today.

The guidance provided by a Rén practice allows us to feel content, knowing that we are doing the best we can and fulfilling our role in this world. By focusing only on our own actions, we remove all distractions outside of our control. As we adapt this practice to our daily lives, treating others with loyalty and honesty, we can spend each day happy and satisfied, without undue anxiety about not being good enough or making mistakes. Being able to continuously learn, understand, apply and change through Rén allows us to meet each day anew with positive action.

I hope that Rén will serve to simplify your life so that you may enjoy every moment more deeply, giving you space and time to appreciate the people and the world around you. I look forward to journeying with you, excited that we will be able to support each other in our quest to improve ourselves, which in turn creates nurturing environments in which we can all thrive.

ACKNOWLEDGEMENTS

My family are the world to me. My mother, father and sister were my first teachers who taught me about life and learning. My strength is from my two grandmothers, my patience from my parents-in-law and every day, I find inspiration and energy to be a better person from the love of my husband and daughter. ♡

Oli, Abi and Amy made this book possible. Thank you.

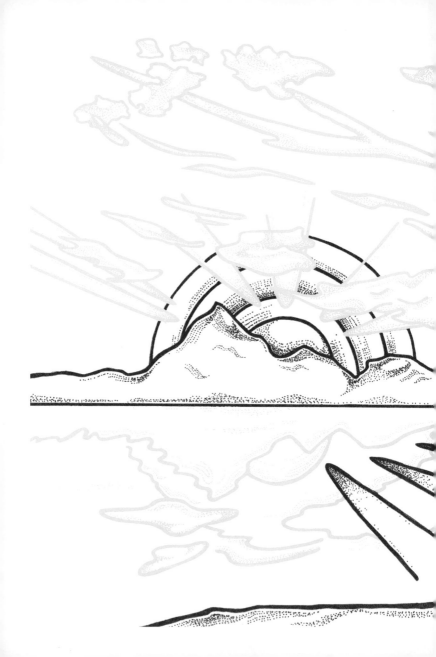

ABOUT THE AUTHOR

Yen Ooi is a writer-researcher who explores East and Southeast Asian culture, identity and values. Her projects aim to cultivate cultural engagement in our modern, technology-driven lives. She is a PhD candidate at Royal Holloway, University of London looking at the development of Chinese science fiction by diaspora writers and writers from Chinese-speaking nations. Her research delves into the critical inheritance of culture that permeates across the genre. Yen is narrative director and writer on *Road to Guangdong*, a narrative-style driving game. She is also author of *Sun: Queens of Earth* (novel) and *A Suspicious Collection of Short Stories and Poetry* (collection). When she's not writing, Yen lectures and mentors. www.yenooi.com